God and the City

Books of Interest from St. Augustine's Press

Robert C. Koons, *Is St. Thomas's Aristotelian Philosophy of Nature Obsolete?*

Kevin Hart, *Contemplation and Kingdom: Aquinas Reads Richard of St. Victor*

Wayne J. Hankey, *Aquinas's Neoplatonism in the Summa Theologiae on God: A Short Introduction*

John F. Boyle, *Master Thomas Aquinas and the Fullness of Life*

Joseph Owens, *Aristotle's Gradations of Being in Metaphysics E–Z*

Robert J. Spitzer, S.J., *Evidence for God from Physics and Philosophy*

Charles P. Nemeth, *Aquinas on Crime*

Peter Kreeft, *An Ocean Full of Angels*

Peter Kreeft, *Summa Philosophica*

Peter Kreef, *The Platonic Tradition*

St. Anselm of Canterbury, *Proslogion*

Fulvio Di Blasi, *From Aristotle to Thomas Aquinas*

Rémi Brague, *Anchors in the Heavens*

James V. Schall, *The Praise of 'Sons of Bitches'*

James V. Schall, *On the Principles of Taxing Beer*

God and the City
An Essay in Political Metaphysics

D. C. Schindler

ST. AUGUSTINE'S PRESS

South Bend, Indiana

Manufactured in the United States of America.

paperback ISBN: 978-1-58731-328-8
ebook ISBN: 978-1-58731-329-5

1 2 3 4 5 6   28 27 26 25 24 23

**Library of Congress Control Number:
2023932004**

Melius Graii atque nostri, qui ut augerent pietatem in deos, easdem illos urbis quas nos incolere voluerunt.
— Cicero, *De legibus*, II.11

"But the Greeks and our ancestors did a better thing: in order that they might increase piety towards the gods, they willed that the gods dwell with us in our cities."

Table of Contents

Table of Contents

Acknowledgments

I would like to thank the Philosophy Department at the University of Dallas for offering me the wonderful opportunity in 2022 to deliver the lecture on which this book was based. The hospitality that the faculty and members of the administration—let me mention especially Jonathan Sanford, Philip Harold, Christopher Mirus, William Frank, Angela Knobel, and Elinor Gardner—showed to me over the course of the visit was exceptional. My gratitude, in particular, goes to Chad Engelland, who tendered the original invitation, and to Matthew Walz, who organized the event while Prof. Engelland was on sabbatical. I would also like to thank Joshua Parens for his lively response to the lecture and his willingness to debate. Finally, I would like to extend a special word of thanks to St. Augustine's Press, and above all to Benjamin Fingerhut, for his patience and graciousness throughout the process of bringing this little book to print.

Introduction

Every distinctive branch of thought, every "science" in the ancient sense of the term, is at bottom an expression of metaphysics, the science of being. This rootedness in metaphysics is implicit in the classical Aristotelian characterization of all the sciences as a study of being in some limited respect: biology, for example, is the study of being specifically in its living form, mathematics is the study of being insofar as it is quantifiable, and so on.[1] To see this is to recognize two things: first, that the various sciences, even in their differentiation into sub-disciplines or specialties, as we call them today, can be related to one another in a proper and fruitful way because these all share a common foundation[2];

---

1   Aristotle,   *Metaph.*,   IV.1.1003a18-32;   cf., VI.1.1025b1-1026a33.
2   For a more elaborate discussion of this point, see D. C. Schindler, "On the Universality of the

second, that the desire to know, which defines human beings, requires us finally to
study that foundation itself; we need to in-
vestigate being, not in one particular respect
or another, but in an unrestricted way: being
as such (*ens qua ens*, τὸ ὂν ᾗ τὸ ὄν, *das Sein
als solches*, being as being). This study of
being as such has traditionally been called
"metaphysics," a title that has not been without controversy, both regarding its prove-
nance and its aptness,[3] to say nothing of the
various objections, especially in postmodern

University: A Response to Jean-Luc Marion,"
Communio (Summer 2013): 77–99.

3 A first-century Peripatetic philosopher, Andron-
icus of Rhodes, gave the name τὰ μετὰ τὰ
φυσικὰ to the unnamed group of texts that
came "after the physics" in the collected edition
of Aristotle's works he published. A question
has persisted whether this designation may be
taken to reveal something of the content of the
science; Kant, for example, believed it was too
fitting to be due merely to chance. For a classic
discussion of the question, see Hans Reiner,
"Die Entstehung und ursprüngliche Bedeutung
des Namens Metaphysik," *Zeitschrift für
philosophische Forschung* 8.2 (1954): 210–37.

thought, to the very notion of a fundamental science.[4]

The significance of the dependence of the various branches of study on metaphysics is not generally acknowledged by contemporary thinkers and rarely reflected on directly even by those who would recognize it in

---

4   The widespread critique of metaphysics, or indeed of Western civilization under the name of "metaphysics," has its most direct roots in Heidegger (see, e.g., his essay "Overcoming Metaphysics," in *The End of Philosophy* [New York: Harper and Row, 1973], 84–110, though it was a constant theme in his middle and later thought) and more indirectly in Nietzsche and Kant. The conception of a "science" called metaphysics has also been debated among Catholic philosophers, especially in the wake of Jean-Luc Marion: see, e.g., Olivier Boulnois, *Métaphysiques rebelles? Genèse et structures d'une science au Moyen Âge* (Paris: PUF, 2013) and *Après la Métaphysique: Augustin?*, ed. Alain de Libera (Paris: Vrin, 2013). In response to postmodern critiques, one often cites Etienne Gilson's quip that the proclamation of the death of metaphysics is always premature: philosophy, he says, specifically with metaphysics in mind, always buries its undertakers.

principle, but will be taken for granted in this little book. Affirming this significance opens up a path for thinking in two directions at once with respect to any given subject matter. On the one hand, if every science is a study of being in a certain respect, we can expect that the nature and essential character of being will have some bearing on the intelligibility of the particular aspect designated by the science. Knowing something about being will cast some light on the particular object of the science, which is, again, not so much a separate thing unto itself as it is an aspect, or a "face," of being. On the other hand, precisely *because* every science presents, as it were, a face of being, and indeed one that is not directly presented in metaphysics itself (as we will explain below), we can also expect that each science will offer some insight, not only into the particular aspect that forms the object of its study, but into being itself. In this regard, a science can be studied in a distinctively philosophical or metaphysical way: we can approach a science with the question, In what distinctive way does this science reveal something about being, about the nature of reality simply?

Our aim in the present work is to engage the science of politics precisely in this way, namely, as a revelation of the meaning of being. But already here we encounter something distinctive about politics, which we will be exploring in a thematic way in this book: politics is not only a particular revelation of being, but a complete one in the practical order, analogous in its comprehensiveness to the theoretical science of metaphysics. What this means, what significance it has, and what it implies in relation to the question of God, will be a basic theme in the following pages.

We are calling this endeavor, not a political *philosophy*, according to the usual terminology, but a political *metaphysics*. This pointed phrase is meant as analogous to "political theology," a phrase made popular by Carl Schmitt last century,[5] but one that has become increasingly common today. Political

5   Carl Schmitt, *Political Theology: Four Chapters on the Concept of Sovereignty* (Chicago: University of Chicago Press, 2006).

theology is an extension into the political sphere of specifically theological concepts or realities. One of the reasons political theology is on the rise today is no doubt the increasingly familiar experience of what we might call political nihilism, the emptiness of the public sphere wherein we enact our lives in common. What prompts the writing of this book is, among other things, a conviction that the immediate conjunction of the theological and the political, while not problematic in principle or absolutely, can be inadequate without a properly philosophical mediation.[6] This inadequacy can become downright dangerous if the combination of politics and theology comes (as it did in Carl Schmitt) in a spirit of reaction to the problems of the age. The absence of philosophy in contemporary political discourse is perhaps most evident in the fact that the ascent

6   This is a fundamental theme in Ferdinand Ulrich's substantial, programmatic essay, "Politische Macht—Philosophie—Gnade," in *Il problema del potere politico. Atti del XVIII. Convegno internaz. del Centro di Studi Filosofici, Gallarete 1963* (Brescia, 1964), 382–501, esp. 384.

of political theology is occurring at the same time as a tendency to reduce "political science" to its more positivist, empirical dimensions and elements. "Political theory," in its classical sense, has all but disappeared from the academy, except perhaps among the relatively closed circle of the followers of Leo Strauss. But, to say it again, we are not seeking to make a contribution to political theory in the sense of philosophizing about some matter or other in the field of politics. Instead, recognizing that this can only be here a first step in what would require much more development, we are aiming to think about politics in relation to its metaphysical ground, as a concrete, publicly enacted, interpretation of being.[7]

---

7   See Ulrich, "Politische Macht," 449, and also Ferdinand Ulrich, "Seinserfahrung und europäische Integration," in *L'unification européenne: Réalité et problèmes. Actes de la Ve Rencontre internat. 1961* (Bozen: Inst. internat. d'études européennes, 1962), 109–10. Note that the proposal we are making here differs from the claim that one cannot do political philosophy without consciously or not making meta-

In short, we intend in the present little book to reflect on, not some political theory or other, nor on the legitimacy of political action or the distinctiveness of particular regimes, but on the nature of political order as such, and how this order implicates the fundamental questions of existence, those concerning man, being, and God. We seek to think about politics *ontologically*. What that means exactly will be explained as we proceed, especially in chapter one.

Before we begin, a comment about the two words in the book's main title are in order. First, God. Although this book engages the question of God in a sustained way, it is important to note that we are not doing so from a *theological* perspective in the strict sense. Instead of starting from an understanding of God enabled by revelation, and thus an understanding specifically in the light of the

physical assumptions: see Jean Hampton, "Should Political Philosophy Be Done Without Metaphysics?" *Ethics* 99.4 (July 1989): 791–814; Ian Adams, "The Inevitability of Political Metaphysics," *Journal of Political Ideology* 4.3 (1999): 269–88.

supernatural gift of faith, we are going to open up the question of God from a more basically metaphysical perspective (which does not mean that we will directly *exclude* the data of revelation): we will be asking after the *being* of political community, and how that being "naturally" implicates the *being* of God. We will be approaching the question of God and politics, one might say, more basically from within the order of creation rather than from within the order of redemption. This is not to say that we are presuming to speak from some neutral place, outside any tradition, on the basis of a putatively pure reason, isolated from faith. Instead, the point is that, even within the ambit of faith, properly understood, reason has a distinctive task in bringing to light the intrinsic nature of things.[8] The approach we take here will be complementary to an eventual political theology in the strict sense, but is nevertheless distinct from it.

---

8   For a longer argument on this score, see my *Companion to Ferdinand Ulrich's Homo Abyssus* (Washington, D.C.: Humanum Academic Press, 2019), 89–112.

As for the word "city": we mean it here simultaneously in a literal, material sense, and in a broader, symbolically extended sense. A city is a compact, regulated gathering of human beings for the purpose of living together in a beneficial way; a city is a *"res publica,"* a "public thing," a unity of existence gathered around "the common." Speaking of its original status, Pierre Manent writes:

> The Greek city was the first complete implementation of human action, the ordering of the human world that made action possible and meaningful, the place where men for the first time deliberated and formulated projects of action. . . . The Greek city was the first form of human life to produce political energy—a deployment of human energy of a new intensity and quality.[9]

9 Pierre Manent, "City, Empire, Church, Nation," in *City Journal*, Summer 2012, at city-journal.org/city-empire-church-nation-13487.html.

The city, which is the actual "prototype" of political life, remains in some respect the fundamental unit of communal human existence—however this unit may evolve over time and in different historical circumstances—and, as such, forms part of our self-understanding and public identity. A city is a realization of "civilization" (as the etymology suggests), and civilization, according to Aquinas, is defined in its absolute sense as common life organized hierarchically under a ruler and regulated by rational laws.[10] It is this basic realization of civilization that Aristotle had in mind when he defined man as a "political animal," that is, a living being whose social nature finds its completion in the "polis," the city; it is this basic unit, likewise, that Plato and, later, Cicero had in mind when they composed their treatises on politics, their respective versions of "The Republic."[11] At a

10 See Aquinas, *Commentary on the Politics*, lesson 1, 23–24.
11 In both cases, the treatise on political order is presented as the founding of a city. Plato's *Politeia*, which might be rendered more literally as

more symbolic level, "the city" can also indicate a way of life or a collective disposition toward reality in general. We see this in studies on the modern way of life (e.g., Harvey Cox's *The Secular City*[12]) and in pop culture ("Sex and the City"), but even more typologically in classical works. The *Ascetic Constitutions*, typically attributed to St. Basil, affirm that Christ offered his life as an "image of the best way of life" (*eikona politeias aristēs*),[13] using a derivative of the word *polis*, "city," to stand for the organization of a common existence. When Augustine wrote of the city of God and the city of man, "city" meant for him a particular ordering of affections—the *ordo amoris*—taken in its communal form. Of course, he *also* meant the actual Church and Rome, both as city and as empire. It is natural to connect the symbolic and the real in this way when one understands politics as an

"the organization of a city," has been translated as "The Republic" in the wake of Cicero.

12 Harvey Cox, *The Secular City* (New York: Macmillan, 1965).

13 *Ascetic Constitutions*, ch. 4, §4, (PG 31, 1351d).

interpretation of being, an embodied and institutionalized claim about the nature of reality.

If we privilege the word "city" in the title, and more generally throughout the present book, as a concrete expression of political existence, understood as enacted order, it is because of the wealth of meaning the little word harbors. This semantic abundance is evident in the word "civilization" that derives from it, in the fact that ancient and medieval discussions of politics favored the word even when they had kingdoms or empires in mind, and in the fact that it us typically used by contemporary studies that seek to recover the depth of the pre-modern tradition in their efforts to make sense of contemporary life, or to pronounce judgment on it: for example, Pierre Manent's *City of Man*,[14] Etienne Gilson's *Metamorphoses of the City of God*,[15] Jacques Ellul's *The Meaning of the*

---

14 Pierre Manent, *The City of Man* (Princeton, NJ: Princeton University Press, 2000).

15 Etienne Gilson, *The Metamorphoses of the City of God* (Washington, DC: CUA Press, 2020).

City,[16] Lewis Mumford's *The City in History*,[17] or Leo Strauss's *The City and Man*.[18] The present book seeks to join, however modestly, in this great and ongoing conversation.

16   Jacques Ellul, *The Meaning of the City*, reprint ed. (Eugene, OR: Wipf and Stock, 2011).
17   Lewis Mumford, *The City in History* (Boston: Mariner Books, 1968).
18   Leo Strauss, *The City and Man* (Chicago: University of Chicago Press, 1978).

Chapter One

"Wie kommt Gott in die Politik?":
The Place of God in the Political Order

In a lecture given in the spring of 1957, which concluded, and attempted to harvest the results from, a course on Hegel's *Science of Logic*, Heidegger posed a fundamental question: Wie kommt Gott in die Philosophie?, "How does God enter into philosophy?"[19] The question is not meant to imply that God at some point stood outside the concern of this fundamental science, and that one day, at some discrete moment, the divine Author of

19 Martin Heidegger, *Identity and Difference* (Chicago: University of Chicago Press, 1969), 55. Translation slightly modified.

all things happened to break into this realm of thought that was initially indifferent to him, which is to say that one thinker or another brought God into his own system of thought for a particular reason of his own devising. Quite to the contrary, even the most superficial perusal of intellectual history reveals that God has always already been implicated in human thinking of a fundamental sort,[20] and that one can scarcely identify a serious philosophy that does not take up the question of God in a direct way and at a decisive moment in its own unfolding.

For his part, Heidegger does not approach intellectual history superficially. One of the basic points of his famous lecture is to show

20   In a classic book, based on his 1936 Gifford Lectures, Werner Jaeger shows that, contrary to common assumptions, philosophy did not originate in ancient Greece with a rejection of religious beliefs in the name of a purified, "secular" reason; rather, Greek philosophy is *saturated* with religion, and is better conceived as the attempt to restore the sense of God in the face of waning popular piety: *The Theology of Early Greek Philosophy*, reprint ed. (Eugene, OR: Wipf and Stock, 2003).

that God is implicated in philosophy as a matter of its very essence, however Heidegger goes on himself to judge that implication. Moreover, he does not raise the question in order to find an immediate answer, which would put an end to that particular question and allow him to move on to others. Instead, he intends to ponder the question, and develop it. The reason he approaches the matter thus is that asking this question properly allows *us* to enter into philosophy ourselves in the most profound way possible, and in doing so to open up, so to speak, the inner essence of philosophy. The question serves this purpose because it brings us to grapple with philosophy's foundations, with both its own most original origin and its highest achievement. The question of God allows thinking to gather itself up as a whole in relation to its origin and end, and in relation to reality as a whole, and conversely it is precisely the reckoning with this relation that allows thinking to gather itself up as a whole: thinking can be a whole only in relation to its origin, and it can relate to its origin properly only as a recollected whole. This is what it means to say that dwelling on and attempting to ask in a serious way, Wie kommt Gott in die Philosophie?, allows the essence of philosophy to come to light. Moreover, because philosophy is human thought in its most concentrated form, to bring to light the essence of philosophy at a given moment in history is to clarify the horizon of thought that defines that particular epoch.

Now, Heidegger has an ulterior motive in raising this question, which will not concern us here. He seeks, by thus entering into and bringing out the essence of philosophy, to reveal God's essential entanglement in philosophical thinking, or in his language, to bring to light the "onto-theo-logical" structure of metaphysics, in order to open up the possibility of an alternative thinking, one that sets God free in relation to thought and thought free in relation to God.[21] Our own purpose in

---

21 See *Identity and Difference*, 72, but also, for example, the "Letter on Humanism," in *Basic Writings* (New York: Harper Perennial, 2008), 251–52. For an attempt to give a positive account of this from a Catholic perspective, see Laurence Paul Hemming, *Heidegger's Atheism: The Refusal of a Theological Voice* (Notre Dame,

beginning with Heidegger is not to present and evaluate his particular interpretation of philosophy, but rather to affirm the depth of his insight and the extraordinary revelatory power of this question, and to raise it in another sphere of human thought, experience, and action, which we will attempt to show is *analogous* to philosophy, as metaphysics, in important ways. Specifically, we wish to ask here, and reflect on, the question, "Wie kommt Gott *in die Politik?*" How does God enter into the political order, into the properly communal organization of human existence? By posing this question, we hope thus to help bring the essence of the political to the fore and to enter into it in a thoughtful way. But in order to raise the question fruitfully, in sharp contrast to Heidegger in this respect, we will draw above all on the sources of the classical Christian—most basically, the Platonic, Aristotelian and Thomistic—tradition.

IN: University of Notre Dame Press, 2007), and my discussion of this attempt in *The Catholicity of Reason* (Grand Rapids, MI: Eerdmans, 2013), 231–61.

The special kinship between metaphysics and politics was established right at the beginning, the moment that the two sciences were first distinguished in their specificity; it is therefore astonishing to consider how rarely this kinship has been observed or explored.[22] One might see the kinship indicated implicitly already in the role of justice and injustice in the constitution of the distinct reality of things in the first extant philosophical fragment,[23] in Parmenides' description of the

22 This is not to say that politics has not been explored from the perspective of metaphysics: see, for example, Dietrich von Hildebrand, *Die Metaphysik der Gemeinschaft* (Regensburg: Josef Habbel Verlag, 1955), or more recently Rocco Buttiglione, *Metaphysics of Knowledge and Politics in Thomas Aquinas* (South Bend, IN: St. Augustine's Press, 2020), and Adrian Pabst, *Metaphysics: The Creation of Hierarchy* (Grand Rapids, MI: Eerdmans, 2012). From a very different perspective, see the ontological reflections on politics in William Desmond, *Ethics and the Between* (Albany, NY: SUNY Press, 2001).

23 The fragment from Anaximander (fr. 1), which appears to be the first extant philosophical text, describes the being of things in the terms of justice and injustice, giving these terms a radically

principal act of being as the unshakeable bond of justice,[24] and in Heraclitus's association of Logos both with the whole of reality and with the law of the city.[25] Certainly, the connection between politics and being appears quite pervasively in Plato's dialogues, most fully no doubt in the *Republic*.[26] But the kinship comes more or less explicitly to the fore in Plato's student Aristotle, who was the first to distinguish the various sciences from each other on the basis of their specific object of study, and to attempt to formulate their

ontological sense just as he interprets being politically. See the discussion of the fragment in Kirk, Raven, and Schofield, *The Presocratic Philosophers*, 2nd ed. (Cambridge: Cambridge University Press, 1983), 100–42, and the much more interesting, if more poetic, interpretation in Friedrich Nietzsche, *Philosophy in the Tragic Age of the Greeks* (Washington, DC: Regnery, 1962).

24   Parmenides, fr. 8, lines 13–15.
25   Heraclitus, frs. 2 and 114.
26   The very fact that what is arguably Plato's most fundamental metaphysics appears in a text devoted to the question of political order merits more reflection that it has been given to date.

relationships to each other in what may be
called a systematic fashion.[27] The multiplicity
of the sciences presents the need for some
principle of unity, a "master" science that lies
at the foundation of all sciences, and thus
serves to gather them together in a meaningful whole—so that we avoid the orderless
"polymathy" that Heraclitus rightly decried
in the ancient world, and the Heraclitean T.
S. Eliot in the modern one.[28] When we inquire
into the unifying principle, however, we

27 We mean "systematic" here in a classic sense
    (i.e., indicating the inter-connectedness of
    things: syn + histanai, being placed together)
    rather than a modern sense (which, following a
    geometrical model, posits as the ideal the logical
    derivation of a whole from a single proposition
    or set of propositions). For a good discussion of
    the modern sense of system, see Robert Spae-
    mann, "Bourgeois Ethics and Non-Teleological
    Ontology," in *The Robert Spaemann Reader* (Ox-
    ford: Oxford University Press, 2015), 55–58.
28 Heraclitus, fr. 16: "Polymathy does not teach
    understanding." T. S. Eliot, in his Choruses
    from *The Rock*, famously laments, "Where is the
    wisdom we have lost in knowledge? Where is
    the knowledge we have lost in information?"

discover, paradoxically, that there is not *one* but two, and that this duality is in some sense irreducible.[29] Because of the fundamental distinction between human thought and human action, and so between *theoretical* science and *practical* science, we ultimately have two master, or "architectonic," sciences, one for each order. The architectonic theoretical science is metaphysics and the architectonic practical science is politics.[30] It is worth noting that this

29   Plato already observes this fundamental difference in *The Statesman*, 258e4-5. On the other hand, Plato proposes, in what appears to be a "per impossibile" mood, the convergence of these two orders in the "philosopher-king" of the *Republic* (V, 473c-d). Is a convergence of this sort a reduction of the two to a simple identity? There is clearly a lot at stake in this question: the collapse of the difference between the theoretical and the practical is arguably the root of all totalitarianism and utopianism, while on the other hand a simple separation between these seems to be the principal cause of nihilism.

30   Aristotle refers to philosophy (as metaphysics) as architectonic in *Metaph.*, I.2.982a14-982b12, and politics as architectonic in *NE* I.2.1094a25-b7. It is interesting to see that, when Aquinas describes metaphysics in these terms, he uses

basic division in the sciences corresponds to
the two classical definitions of man, which
stem from Aristotle: man is the *rational* (i.e.,
"metaphysical") animal,[31] and man is the *political* animal.[32] We will discuss these definitions in the next chapter.

Aristotle defines the architectonic theoretical science—which we call "metaphysics"
but he called "first philosophy" or "theology"[33]—as the "science of being," which
studies the principal qualities of being and
its causes.[34] Whereas all the other sciences
study being in a certain respect, metaphysics
studies being qua being, which is to say

an essentially political metaphor: metaphysics
is the ruler or regulator (rectrix, regulatrix): see
his prologue to the *Commentary on Metaphysics*.

31 Aristotle, *NE*, I.13. It is worth noting that Aristotle does not explicitly use the expression "rational animal," but it is clearly implied as the
point of this chapter in the *Ethics* and has been
attributed to Aristotle no doubt by analogy to
his expression "*zoon politikon*."

32 Aristotle, *Politics*, I.2.1253a1.

33 Aristotle, *Metaph.*, IV.2.1004a2-4 and *Metaph.*
VI.1.1026a18-23.

34 Aristotle, *Metaph.*, IV.1.1003a18-33.

simpliciter or ἁπλῶς. Because there is nothing at all without some share in being, we can say that, in studying being in this unrestricted way, metaphysics studies the whole of reality[35]; it excludes nothing in principle, or, to speak more precisely, it does not even exclude nothing, since, as Aristotle observes, we understand even non-being with respect to being to the extent that we say that non-being *is*.[36] It is crucial to note, however, that metaphysics studies the whole of reality, not in a collective sense, in every detail, one after the other, but in what we might call a "metaphysical" sense: it studies everything specifically with respect to being. This is why

35 See Aristotle, *Metaph.*, IV.2.1004b1.
36 Aristotle, *Metaph.*, IV.2.1003b10-12. We might compare Aristotle's reference to non-being, which gives priority to being, to Heidegger's insistence on their equiprimordiality in "What is Metaphysics?," *Basic Writings* (San Francisco: Harper Perennial, 2008), 93–110. Ferdinand Ulrich attempts to accommodate Heidegger's argument within a more ample interpretation of Thomistic metaphysics: *Homo Abyssus: The Drama of the Question of Being* (Washington, DC: Humanum Academic Press, 2018), 28–46.

metaphysics does not absorb the other, specific sciences[37]; nor is it identical to the collected sum of all the sciences in their particularity.[38] Instead, we could say that it grounds the other sciences by clarifying their unifying object and ontologically establishing their distinctive objects in each case. In this sense, perhaps contrary to common impressions, metaphysics is what allows each of the sciences to be genuinely concrete, revealing the precise way each of the sciences speaks about *reality*—a common reality in

---

37 Monte Ransome Johnson begins his discussion of "Aristotle's Architectonic Sciences" with the apt statement, "Aristotle rejected the idea of a single, overarching super-science or 'theory of everything,' and he presented a powerful and influential critique of scientific unity," *Theory and Practice in Aristotle's Natural Science*, ed. David Ebrey (Cambridge: Cambridge University Press, 2015), 163.

38 See Aristotle, *Metaph.*, III.4.999a24-29, in which Aristotle explains that the universal scope of first philosophy cannot mean knowledge of all individual things as individual, for "how is it possible to get knowledge of the infinite individuals?"

which they all meet each other, so to speak, from their irreducibly different places.[39]

Let us reflect on this point for a moment, because it will prove to be crucial for the proper interpretation of politics. Although math and biology, for example, study being in a particular respect (qua quantifiable or qua living), to study being itself is not to learn math and biology; their objects are not simply reducible to being—which is, incidentally, why being is so thoroughly *analogical*. Indeed, one might even say that studying math or biology, precisely because of their irreducible specificity, offers an insight into being that is not available directly to metaphysics.[40] At the same

39 It is good to keep in mind, contrary to popular imagination, that philosophy, far from being abstract, is the most concrete discourse that there is. Hegel made this argument in a decisive (if somewhat sarcastic) way two centuries ago: "Who Thinks Abstractly?," *Hegel: Text and Commentary* (Garden City, NY: Anchor Books, 1966), 113–18.

40 We might compare this point to Aquinas's notion of the transcendental properties, each of which is the same as being "in reality," but nevertheless introduces an aspect that is not present in the understanding of being itself. In this case,

time, however, metaphysics matters to these distinct sciences: On the one hand, it gives an ontological depth and substantial reality to what might otherwise become a pure abstraction—we might consider here, for example, the remarkable study of Jacob Klein comparing the (metaphysically-grounded) Greek and the early modern concept of number, and the increasingly prevalent recognition of what a retrieval of the notion of substantial form (brought to the fore in metaphysics) can contribute to the understanding of biological life.[41] On the other hand, a sense of being and its essentially ontological character can give weight

though nothing can be added to being in one respect, in another respect each of the transcendental properties can be said to "add" something that is not in being itself: see, for example, Aquinas, *De ver.* 1.1 and 21.1; cf., ST 1.5.1ad1. If this is true about those properties closest to being, and as comprehensive as being, it is also true for notions of a lower level.

41 Jacob Klein, *Greek Mathematical Thought and the Origin of Algebra* (Massachusetts: MIT Press, 1976); Marjorie Grene, "Aristotle and Modern Biology," in *Journal of the History of Ideas* 33.3 (1972): 395-424. See the more recent (and more

and an ontological foundation to the specificity of the sciences, keeping us from reducing biology to math, or math to psychology, for example. On this score, it warrants mention that the particular interpretation of being bears profoundly on this point: a Heideggerian sense arguably threatens to eclipse the distinctive sciences, whereas a Thomistic/Aristotelian sense decidedly does not.[42] In a word, metaphysics does not compete with or otherwise replace the sciences that fall under it, but, precisely to the contrary, allows them to be fully

polemical) argument on behalf of the importance of Aristotle in modern science by Edward Feser, *Aristotle's Revenge: The Metaphysical Foundations of the Physical and Biological Sciences* (Neuenkirchen-Seelscheid, Germany: Editiciones Scholasticae, 2019).

42 Although he protested the charge, Heidegger was regularly criticized for eclipsing the sciences, whether natural or human, by the brilliant darkness of being as such: see his "Letter on Humanism," 249–50; cf., A. J. Wendland, "Heidegger vs. Kuhn: Does Science Think?," in *Heidegger on Technology*, ed. Wendland, Merwin, and Hadjioannou (Oxfordshire: Routledge, 2018), 282–98.

themselves. Metaphysics, properly inter-preted, *liberates* the other sciences, giving them substance, grounding their irreducible unique-ness in a way that they themselves can only take for granted.[43]

How, then, does God enter into this pic-ture, that is, into the study of being qua being? Wie kommt Gott in die Philosophie? Clearly, if metaphysics studies the whole of reality, and doesn't exclude nothing, then it cannot but also include God, at least in some respect. It is just its fundamental and all-encompass-ing character that makes this inclusion

---

43 Aquinas argues that no particular science deter-mines the existence or essence of its subject mat-ter, but takes the essence for granted and unfolds its intelligibility; but metaphysics *does* determine essence and existence. We can inter-pret this as saying that metaphysics grounds the other particular sciences: see Aquinas *Commen-tary on Metaphysics*, VI, lectio 1, 1152. For a pow-erful account of how a robust notion of *esse*, especially as illuminated by the doctrine of cre-ation, founds the integrity of the sciences in their irreducible distinctness and integrity, see Michael Hanby, *No God, No Science* (Oxford: Wiley-Blackwell, 2013), esp., 334–74.

inevitable.[44] The decisive question is therefore
not *whether* metaphysics includes God, but *on
what terms*, so to speak, it includes God. Heidegger, evidently drawing on Aristotle's discussion in the *Metaphysics*,[45] even if he does
not make it explicit in this context, argues that
metaphysics includes God specifically as presenting being in its *highest* sense.[46] If reason,
in metaphysics, seeks the meaning of being,

---

44 See Edith Stein's perceptive observation in this
    regard in *Finite and Eternal Being* (Washington,
    DC: ICS Publications, 2002), 21–23.

45 *Metaph.*, I.2.982b27-983a11; cf., *Metaph.*, IV.1-
    2.1003a18-1003b19 and *Metaph.* VI.1.1025b1-
    1026a34.

46 Heidegger, *Identity and Difference*, 70–71; cf., "In-
    troduction to 'What is Metaphysics?,'" in *Path-
    marks* (Cambridge: Cambridge University
    Press, 1998), 287. For Heidegger, this is precisely
    why metaphysics is not able to ask the question
    of being as such (see "Letter on Humanism,"
    Basic Writings, 247). Assuming (without ques-
    tioning) the sense of being as "the brightest," so
    to speak, it fails to take heed of being's essential
    concealment, which belongs inseparably to its
    disclosure. To think this, for Heidegger, requires
    a radically different starting point from that
    given in traditional thought.

Heidegger explains, it seeks it in its most fundamental and general sense, and so comes to rest in ontology; but it also finds illumination of the meaning of being in its supreme instance, namely, God, and so it comes to rest in theology. This, in a very brief nutshell, is why, according to Heidegger, metaphysics is constitutionally "onto-theo-logical."

But if Heidegger is right regarding *Aristotle's* metaphysics—and we will leave that question open[47]—it must be said that Aristotle is not the only thinker who interpreted the relationship between God and being; there is also the radically new light cast on the matter through the Christian notion of *creatio ex nihilo*,[48] not to mention the significantly different view formulated in

---

47 Thomas Joseph White is no doubt right to criticize Heidegger's interpretation of Aristotle, but it is not clear that he himself has a proper grasp of Heidegger's argument: see his *Wisdom in the Face of Modernity* (Naples, FL: Ave Maria Press, 2016), and my extended discussion of his argument in *Catholicity of Reason*, 262–304.

48 Kenneth Schmitz, *The Gift: Creation* (Milwaukee, WI: Marquette University Press, 1982).

Plotinus and the neoplatonic tradition that was taken up into Christian reflection.[49] Without entering into a discussion of the development of this tradition, and the spectrum of different views in the Middle Ages on its implications for the relation of metaphysics and God, we can say that the key conceptual point lies in Aristotle's statement that metaphysics studies being in its fundamental attributes *and its first causes*.[50] If God enters into the purview of metaphysics, thus defined, it is not because he is the biggest or best or highest being *within the horizon of the world of beings*, but because he is the radically transcendent cause of that world, and of everything within its horizon without exception.[51]

---

49 On this point, see Norris Clarke, "The Limitation of Act by Potency," in *The New Scholasticism* 26.2 (1952): 167–94. It is worth noting that Heidegger notoriously neglects this tradition in his account of the "history of being."

50 *Metaph.*, IV.1.1003a31-32: "It is of being as being that we must grasp the first causes."

51 This does not mean that the metaphysician takes God simply as the perfect representative of being in its most complete sense, already fin-

Christian thought recognizes what has come to be called the *analogical* difference between God and being. This implies a dramatic shift in perspective: we do not first establish the horizon of the meaning of being and then find God simply within that horizon—which is to say that metaphysics does not reduce simply to ontology. But nor do we simply start with God and derive the meaning of the world's being directly from him, which is to say that metaphysics does not reduce to theology. Metaphysics is not just ontology or theology, nor is it simply the combination of the two. Instead, the word "drama" is especially fitting here: *being* sets the horizon for the study that came to be called metaphysics, but God breaks into that horizon from above, so to speak, rather than lying wholly within the horizon as if that were the more comprehensive setting. The relation is dramatic because metaphysics thus

ished existing, so to speak, and thus fails to ask the more radical question of the *meaning* of being.

includes what lies in some basic sense beyond its scope. There is no simple opposition, here, between openness and closure, such as one finds in the Levinasian critique of "totality"[52]: the study of being has to be already complete, as a horizon, in order to allow God to break in, and it is against the backdrop of what transcends it that this study can *be* a horizon and so be complete. God *is* indeed being in its highest sense, but that sense is strictly *analogical*. God is not merely inside the horizon of being (as Heidegger suggests in his identifying of metaphysics with ontotheology), nor merely outside the horizon of being (as Jean-Luc Marion, for example, has famously argued in his critical response to Heidegger[53]), but always both at once. To use the language that Erich Przywara developed in his formulation of the *analogia entis*, we could say that God is *both in and*

52 Emmanuel Levinas, *Totality and Infinity* (Pittsburgh: Duquesne University Press, 1969).
53 Jean-Luc Marion, *God Without Being* (Chicago: University of Chicago Press, 1991), 53–107.

beyond the horizon of being.[54] In this respect, reason, which of its very nature and essence aspires to the meaning of being, is carried naturally beyond itself; it opens from within itself to what lies in a radical way beyond itself, which is to say reason naturally opens to faith.[55] Thus transformed, metaphysics, far from being constitutively onto-theo-logical, opens up from within itself, precisely *as* the study of being, to theology as a *radically distinct* science (even as theology opens naturally to metaphysics, since the self-revealing God it studies is the ultimate cause

---

54 Erich Przywara, *Analogia Entis: Metaphysics, Original Structure, and Universal Rhythm* (Grand Rapids, Mich.: Eerdmans, 2014), 190.

55 This is the principal point of John Paul II's *Fides et Ratio* (1998). Note that to say that reason opens naturally to faith is decidedly not to say that faith is simply natural to reason or represents its natural object. The supernatural object of faith essentially transcends reason, but this essential transcendence is further complexified, so to speak, in history by sin: for some interesting reflections along these lines, see Robert Spaemann, "The Traditionalist Error," in *The Spaemann Reader*, 37–44.

of being, and so the exemplar of all that is[56]). In a word, God is not the object of metaphysics, but in some sense inevitably "enters into" that object as its transcendent cause, which means that what God reveals about himself is neither built into the essence of metaphysics by definition and in an *a priori* way, nor is it merely accidental to that essence, but it illuminates the inner essence of metaphysics with a light that transcends metaphysics.[57]

It may seem that we have long left the path of inquiry into our principal theme, namely, God and the city, but it will become clear shortly that the details of our formulation of the relation between God and metaphysics bears directly on our interpretation of politics from this fundamental perspective. To see this, we must first recall the kinship we observed between politics and

---

56 Aquinas *ST* 1.44.3.
57 To make this point from a variety of angles is the aim of the essays in *The Catholicity of Reason* (Grand Rapids, Mich.: Eerdmans, 2013), especially the essay entitled "Surprised by Truth: The Drama of Reason in Fundamental Theology," 35–57.

metaphysics.[58] Let us dwell on this for a moment. Metaphysics is the master science in the theoretical order because it studies the most fundamental and comprehensive object there is, namely, being qua being. Politics, by analogy, is the master science in the practical order because it concerns what we might describe as the most comprehensive sphere of

58　The intertwining of the two is deeper and more intricate than we can explore here: metaphysics, even as the master theoretical science, is defined as aiming ultimately, not at the true, but at the good (*Metaph.*, I.1.982b4-10), and the highest human happiness, which governs the practical order, is most essentially contemplation (*NE* X.7.1177a6-1178a8). Even more subtly and intrinsically, the highest moment of the human community of friendship, for Aristotle, is the enjoyment of one another's *being* (*NE* IX.9.1170b1-1170b13), and, conversely, the created act of being in its ultimate sense is a communal act (see Aquinas on *esse commune*, but also on the diversity of the cosmos as expressing the simplicity of God: ST 1.47.1). Also, Aquinas presents metaphysics as *ruling* the other sciences, and explains its role by comparing it to a good ruler: see his *Prologue* to the *Commentary on Metaphysics*.

human existence. As Aristotle explains in the
opening sentences of the *Politics*:

> Every city (πόλιν) is a community
> (κοινωνίαν) of some kind, and
> every community is established
> with a view to some good. But, if
> all communities aim at some
> good, the state or political com-
> munity, which is the highest of all,
> and which embraces all the rest
> (πάσας περιέχουσα τὰς ἄλλας),
> aims at good in a greater degree
> than any other, and at the highest
> good.[59]

Just as human action aims inevitably at some
good,[60] so too the ordered *inter*-action of
human beings, to the extent that it is indeed
the inter-related actions of individual human
beings (and not just an accidental coincidence of discrete acts), aims at a *common
good*.[61] The different kinds of communities,

59 *Politics*, 1.1252a1-7.
60 *NE* I.1.1094a1-2.
61 *NE* I.2.1094a17-1094b11. It is worth noting that

then, are specified by the different aspects
of the human good they are meant to realize
in common. Now, just as the characterization of the variety of sciences as the study of
being in a certain respect leads to the need
for a science of being as such and not only
in a certain limited respect, so too does the
characterization of human community as
ordered to the good in a certain respect lead
to the need for a human community ordered
to the good as such, without specifying

Aristotle avoids speaking of a "common good"
in his discussion in the *Politics*, using instead the
expression "common interest." See Mark Shiff-
man's discussion of this point ("Human Good,
Political Good, Common Good: The City of God
as the Unattainable Truth of Political Community," unpublished PMR paper). It is not entirely
clear why he does so, but one possible reason is
Aristotle's decisive rejection of Plato's notion of
the "good as such" in contrast to goodness in an
always relative sense—i.e., good for this or that
particular thing, or individual. But the Christian
tradition has no such reservations regarding the
"transcendental" sense of goodness as such;
Aquinas, in his *Commentary on the Politics*, simply assumes that Aristotle is speaking of the
"bonum commune": see, e.g., book 1, lectio 1, 11.

qualification, the *whole human good*.[62]
Aquinas brings out even more strongly the
completeness of the good that defines politics: "If every society is ordered to a good,
that society which is the highest necessarily
seeks in the highest degree the good that is
the highest among all human goods . . . and
so political society is itself the highest society."[63] This complete human community is
what Aristotle calls the *city*, the "polis"—
which is sometimes translated in this context
into English as "the state" or the "city-state,"

---

62 According to Aquinas, "the highest [human so-
ciety] is that of a city, which is ordered to the
satisfaction of all the needs of human life.
Hence of all human societies this is the most
perfect [*perfectissima*]," Prologue, *Commentary on
Politics*, 4. The notion of "perfect society" or
"community" underwent an evolution over the
course of history, but in Aquinas the phrase
clearly designates the completeness of a society,
which is to say the comprehensiveness of the
good around which the society is ordered. As
we will explain below, "comprehensive" in this
context does not mean comprehensive in every
respect (*totus sed non totaliter*).

63 *Commentary on Politics*, lectio 1, 11.

because we naturally think of a city, not so much as a supreme political entity unto itself (in spite of the fact that the very word "politics" means, literally, "city matters"), but as a part of a larger unity, typically the nation.

This ambiguity, the difficulty that presents itself in translating the term "polis," deserves attention. We tend to distinguish between "city" and "state" principally in quantitative terms. But the crucial consideration regarding completeness or perfection for Aristotle is not the size of the political unity or community,[64] but its status in the order of goodness. Specifically, the crucial point is its *comprehensiveness*, its capacity to include within itself the ends pursued by other societies, such as the household or the village—indeed, in a manner that we will have to specify below, also the society of the Church. Before addressing that, let us speculatively deepen the point about what precisely defines what Aquinas calls the "most

64 Though this *does* concern him: see *Politics*, VII.6.1327a13-1327b19.

perfect" (*perfectissima*) society of the city. Human beings cannot but pursue what they take to be good, both in each discrete action and in their lives as a whole, so that an individual life can be taken to be an interpretation, whether conscious and deliberate or not, of what the human good *is*. The organization of human life in a community, beyond the regulation of discrete actions, or, in other words, a city, is thus inevitably itself a particular interpretation of the highest human good.[65] Just as one cannot study any particular science, understood as a study of being in a particular respect, without (however unconsciously) taking for granted or implying a metaphysics, that is, an interpretation of the meaning of being as such, so too one cannot have a human community that is not an interpretation of *the* human

65 Intriguingly, Aquinas says that the city is a "conjecture" (coniectatrix) concerning the highest human good, meaning in this context that it projects a particular conception of that good, around which it is organized: see *Commentary on the Politics*, Book 1, Lectio 1 [11]."

good, as such.[66] Whatever human community thus sets the ultimate horizon for the unfolding of human life, *that* community is the one properly designated as the *polis*. With such a robust notion of the *polis* in the background, Michael Oakeshott has thus poignantly expressed the way in which philosophy and politics mirror each other in their effort at comprehensiveness:

> Probably there has been no theory of the nature of the world, of the activity of man, of the destiny of mankind, no theology or cosmology, perhaps even no metaphysics, that has not sought a reflection of itself in the mirror of political philosophy; certainly there has been no fully considered politics that

---

66 As Aristotle makes clear in the *Ethics*, different habitual orders of life imply different interpretations of what is good (*NE* I.8). We can infer from this that the perfect community of a city, which is ordered to the highest good in the highest degree, will therefore imply an interpretation of the highest good.

has not looked for its reflection in
eternity.[67]

The city is the political entity that sets the
boundaries of the good that defines man, in
the sense that it identifies the highest good in
the highest degree. The city, in other words, is
the place wherein man lives in both a physical
and a metaphysical sense, so to speak; it is
that which opens up the space wherein his life
may unfold in relation to others. But that
space will always and in every case be concrete, characterized by a certain *ethos*. The argument regarding what constitutes a city,
properly understood, is an essential one, de-
termined by the logic of the matter, rather
than a merely historically contingent one. It
may be that, for the Greeks of the classical period, the relatively small but more or less self-
contained city of Athens, or Sparta, or Thebes,

67 Michael Oakeshott, "Introduction," in Thomas
    Hobbes, *Leviathan, or the Matter, Forme and Power
    of a Commonwealth Ecclesisticall and Civil*, ed.
    Michael Oakeshott (Oxford: Basil Blackwell,
    1946), vii–lxvi, cited in Francis Oakley, "Politics
    & Eternity," *Daedalus* 143.1 (Winter 2014): 35–36.

represented the most fundamental and comprehensive political unit; nevertheless, if we view the matter in relation to its principle, we may say that any and every people, organized *as* a people, at any particular moment in history, will be part of a fundamental political community that represents (successfully or unsuccessfully) the complete human good. The community that represents the complete good is a *polis*, the actual reality that is intended when we speak in general terms of the "political order." It is worth emphasizing this point because the world we inhabit, and which informs our imagination, not only denies it but is in fact fundamentally characterized by this denial: what essentially defines the modern world is a *separation* of the political from the comprehensive human good (or more specifically an inevitably frustrated effort to effect this separation).[68] We will come

68   The classic expression of this is of course the position articulated by John Rawls, *A Theory of Justice*, 2nd ed. (Cambridge, MA: Harvard, 1999), who defines the political *specifically* as excluding comprehensive doctrines of the good, which belong thus to the private sphere of civil society.

back to this point at the end. For now, we need to see that politics cannot help but be about the ultimate meaning of life. This is just what it means to say that politics is the architectonic science in the practical order.

Now, just as the comprehensiveness of the object of metaphysics necessarily opens it up in a dramatic fashion, in an indirect but at the same time *intrinsic* way, to theology, so too does the comprehensiveness of politics open *it* up to God. Before we explore how it does, however, we will propose a certain modification of Aristotle's characterization in a way that will bear fruit later in our discussion. As we have seen, Aristotle identified metaphysics and politics as the two architectonic sciences, one in the theoretical and the other in the practical order. But to characterize politics as a science, though true and illuminating, runs the risk of our conceiving politics most basically in theoretical terms, even if we qualify it as a

---

The more subtle formulation he offers in his later work (see *Political Liberalism*, expanded ed. [New York: Columbia University Press, 2005]) does not alter this fundamental point.

practical science, and thus of our failing to grasp the significance of the difference between the theoretical and the practical orders, between the true and the good.[69] According to Aristotle, while the conclusion of a theoretical syllogism is a proposition, the conclusion of a practical syllogism is not a proposition, as we might think, especially if we think of it is as science—"X ought to be done"; instead, a practical syllogism concludes in an actual *decision*, or indeed an action.[70] The good at which practical reason aims is not simply an object of understanding, but a reality: "the end aimed

69 Monte Ransome Johnson argues that politics is ultimately subordinate to metaphysics: "Aristotle's Architectonic Sciences," 163–86, but, while this may be true in an absolute and abstract sense, it is crucial to see that there remains what we might call an incommensurability, insofar as they define two irreducibly different orders of being.

70 Combining *De anima*, III.11.434a15-20 and *NE* VII.3.1147a25-30. See Alasdair MacIntyre's well-known discussion of this point and the (debatable) contrast he presents with Augustine: *Whose Justice? Which Rationality?* (Notre Dame, IN: University of Notre Dame Press, 1988), 124–63.

at [by political science] is not knowledge but action."[71] As Aquinas puts this point from Aristotle, while truth lies in the mind, goodness lies "in rebus," in real things.[72] In short, a "practical science" is not a science in the sense of a reflective appropriation of its object (though of course includes just that), but ultimately a *doing*, a realization of the good in the concrete order, in reality. Given this difference, there would seem to be good reason to say that the specifically political analogue to reason in metaphysics is not so much practical reason as it is the actual enactment of practical reason specifically with respect to the comprehensive common good, which is to say the ordering of the community to its proper end. In a word, the political analogue to metaphysical reason would seem to be *authority*.

Before proceeding to draw inferences from this analogy between (practical) authority and (theoretical) reason, it is necessary to make a further distinction. Opening up to the practical order *as* practical, and not

71   NE, I.3.1095a4-5.
72   Aquinas, *De ver.*, 21.1.

simply as (theoretical) science, introduces a dimension that is essential to politics, but will not be part of the "political metaphysics" we are proposing here, except incidentally. To speak of an act that aims at realizing the good is to open up the possibility of failure; indeed, as Plato observes in the *Republic*, the effort to realize an intention in the practical order *always* falls short in some respect.[73] For this reason, politics is never simply about establishing order, but is also, and indeed in a fundamental way, about managing disorder. It is not accidental that classical political philosophy has been concerned with *protecting* the community— which means, on the one hand, exercising power in a coercive sense with respect to disorder (*ad intra*), and, on the other hand, forming and training a military force in the face of threats from other polities (*ad extra*). To posit a political aim without acknowledging and preparing for the real possibility—or indeed, better put, the possibility that necessarily accompanies the movement into the

73   Plato, *Rep.* V, 473a-b.

real order—of failure and disorder, and thus to collapse the theoretical and practical orders into one, is to establish a kind of metaphysical violence—and eventually also a political violence. This is the kernel of truth in Leo Strauss's well-known interpretation of Plato's *Republic*.[74] At the same time, however, it is crucial not to allow disorder to set the horizon of politics, and so, quite literally, to define it. This problem, namely, the definition of politics as the purely practical endeavor to manage disorder, has taken a great variety of forms in history: from a certain interpretation of Augustine's *City of God*, to Machiavelli, to modern social contract theory, to Weber's definition of sovereignty as the possession of a monopoly on coercive power, to Carl Schmitt's claim that politics is founded on the friend-enemy distinction. By describing the approach we are taking in this book as a "political metaphysics," we mean to view politics as *praxis* (and not simply as *theōria*), but at the same time to view *praxis*—all *praxis*, in fact, but paradigmatically

74 Strauss, *City and Man.*

politics as what we might call the "most perfect" *praxis*—specifically as a revelation of being. We are thus looking at politics most fundamentally as a realization of meaning, one might say, but as always having to reckon in a *real* way with failure. The point is that this failure can only be properly understood as a failure to be what politics actually is, a privileged revelation of being.

Let us now turn to the analogy we proposed between theoretical reason and political authority. This analogy is richer than one might initially think; reflecting upon the two reveals an extraordinary complementarity, and begins a proper response to the question, Wie kommt Gott in die Politik? As we have seen, reason, in seeking to understand, seeks the meaning of being, and this search opens it up to God as the ultimate "First Cause" of being, which ultimately means as *Ipsum Esse Subsistens*. There is here a kind of *ascent* of reason, an *ana*-logos, from the world up into God, though of course this itinerary must not be understood in a dualistic fashion, in the sense that we first have an understanding of the world and then

after that we grasp God.[75] Authority seems
to move in the opposite direction: the word
"authority" is derived etymologically from
"author," "auctor," which means the origi-
nator of an order. The supreme author is of
course God, and traditional cultures have ac-
cordingly always recognized the sacred
character of authority, its rootedness in the
divine, ultimately in God. (We will be devel-
oping this point at greater length in the two
chapters that follow.) A person who has authority, then, represents this transcendent
principle to a particular community and in
so doing communicates order. In complementary contrast to metaphysical reason,
political authority exhibits something of a
descending, a "kata-logical," motion, from
God to the world.[76] The gaze of the authority,

---

75 See my discussion of this in *Catholicity of Reason*,
    305–33.
76 We might think, here, of Plato's allegory of the
    cave, the *philosopher*, who has ascended *from* the
    cave, becomes the philosopher *king*, i.e., a
    specifically political authority, in his descent
    back into the cave, into which he is meant to
    bring the light of the good (*Rep.*, VII, 520b-d).

though drawing on the highest light available, is in a sense directed all the way unto the lowest of things, in an effort to help even these to be expressions of the life-giving order originating in God. The deeper etymological root of the word "authority" is "augere," to augment, increase, or make grow. It belongs to the very essence of authority, by representing the Author, to bring about the flourishing of all things under him, just as the light of the sun causes plants, and in some sense all beings, to grow.[77]

By analogy to metaphysical reason, which is inevitably fundamental and comprehensive insofar as it cannot but form some notion of being whether it wills to or not,[78] political authority is inevitably fundamental and

We might compare this also to the complementarity, within the theoretical order, between philosophy and theology (*Catholicity of Reason*, 305–33).

77   Plato, *Republic*, VI, 509b.

78   Aquinas, *De ver.*, 1.1: being is "quod primo intellectus concipit quasi notissimum"; it is moreover "illud quod primo cadit in apprehensione" (*ST* 1-2.94.2) and "quod primus cadit in conceptione intellectus" (*ST* 1.5.2).

comprehensive in the practical order: it cannot help but realize, or pretend to realize, the whole human good in the highest degree whether it will or no, just because it is the supreme ordering principle of human life. To anticipate an obvious objection, there are two decisive reasons that this notion of political authority as fundamental and comprehensive is not essentially "totalitarian." The first is analogous to the reason metaphysics does not absorb the other sciences, but founds them and their independence. To enact political community as authority is not to undertake each and every activity that constitutes human life; authority is about the whole, but precisely *not* in the collective sense. It is instead about establishing the horizon, so to speak, wherein each activity, as a relatively independent order, can have its proper place, which is to say a place that belongs specifically to that activity in its relatively autonomous integrity and at the same time in a manner that connects it to all the others.[79] Just as metaphysics gives an

---

79 See my essay, "The Sources of Authority," in *New Polity*, (Spring 2022): 17-23.

ontological depth to each distinct science without eclipsing that science's distinctness, political authority enables each human activity to be a particular realization of, and contribution to, the common good, which is to say a distinctive expression of the meaning of human existence. The completeness of the political good does not imply the eclipse or the extrinsic management of the various goods and the particular societies that realize them below it; instead, their inclusion as real goods, which occurs by virtue of the effective principle of authority, is just what gives them their substantial independence.[80] In

80 According to Aquinas, "man is not ordained to the body politic, according to all that he is and has" (*ST* 1-2.21.4ad3). Aquinas moreover maintains a distinction between natural law and positive law (unlike Hegel), but (arguably unlike Hobbes and Locke) without separating them as simply extrinsic to each other. Instead, there is a paradox in Aquinas's view: human order can bring the natural order to its completion without eliminating its natural (and in that respect "extra-cultural or political") character. The paradox is that that which stands outside of culture flourishes most properly within it, and that it is

this sense, real authority is by its very nature generative of what Catholic Social Teaching has called "subsidiarity," which is to say the liberation of proper authorities within each distinct sphere of activity.

The second reason the comprehensiveness of authority is not "totalitarian" is that the political good, precisely *as* comprehensive, opens up beyond itself, not only to what lies below it, but at the same time (and arguably for the very same reason) to what lies above it. To see this, let us finally turn to face directly the basic question that has framed this chapter, Wie kommt Gott in die Politik? It may seem that we have already answered this question: the political authority is meant to represent God to the

precisely within culture that the natural distinguishes itself as natural. We will see how this same paradox is reflected in the body-soul relation as Aquinas interprets it. One of the paradigmatic expressions of this paradox is Aquinas's interpretation of private property, which is in some sense natural even while it is not given in nature: see Hermann Chroust and Robert J. Affeldt, "The Problem of Private Property According to St. Thomas Aquinas," *Marquette Law Review* 34.3 (Winter 1950-51): 151–82.

people and thus to communicate the divine order to the community. God is therefore in politics from the beginning, insofar as all authority derives from him, as St. Paul said.[81] But we have yet to specify exactly how God is present, and exactly what this means for the nature of political order. We will be working out aspects of this in the second and third chapters here, but we can still make a basic point in the last part of this chapter. It turns out that the analogy with metaphysical reason is illuminating also on this score. As we saw above, God is not the object of metaphysics in a direct way, but only in an indirect sense, as the cause of its formal object, which is being as such. This is why there is a *difference* between metaphysics and theology, a difference that can be radicalized according to the principle of analogy and in the light of God's absolute freedom with respect to the world implied in the notion of *creatio ex nihilo*. For similar reasons, we may say that God is not the immediate object of politics, which is to say that God is not, without qualification, the common good that defines the political community

81   *Romans* 13:1.

as such.[82] Again, because of the special character of divine revelation and because of the
specificity of the community directly founded
in and through Jesus Christ in view of the eschaton, we need to recognize a difference between the Church and the political order,
which is analogous to the difference between
theology and metaphysics.

It bears remarking that there is an important sense in which the Church is meant to *include* the political order: indeed, the whole
cosmos is ultimately meant to be incorporated
into the body of Christ, when the Son of God
will be "all in all." In this respect, the Church
is not divided against the political order as two

82 Charles de Koninck, "On the Primacy of the
    Common Good against the Personalists," *The
    Aquinas Review* 4 (1997): 11–70. De Koninck
    makes a strong argument for God as the com-
    mon good in (implicit) response to Jacques Mar-
    itain, who insists on separating God from the
    political common good (see *The Person and the
    Common Good* [Notre Dame, IN: University of
    Notre Dame Press, 1966], 62–64, 71–75). Our ar-
    gument differs from both, but we are closer to
    de Koninck in the rejection of Maritain's ten-
    dency to privatize the highest good.

different entities or communities, but is itself the whole. Nevertheless, the Church is an essentially analogous reality; affirming the comprehensive character of the Church does not eliminate in another respect the distinction between *ecclesia* and *polis*. The matter is similar to the one we will elaborate in chapter three: just as the soul in one sense *contains* the body, it is also radically different from the body in another sense, such that it is necessary to speak of the *relation* between body and soul. Similarly, the comprehensiveness of the Church in one respect does not eclipse the difference between Church and polis, such that we may speak of their *relation* in the temporal order.

There are two obvious objections to the interpretation of politics we have been proposing here, each of which comes from a distinct direction. The first is that the insistence on the comprehensive character of political society betrays the "Gelasian dyarchy" that represents what is properly distinctive in Christian political thought.[83] According to

83 The traditional claim has recently been repeated by William McCormick, *The Christian Structure*

Pope Gelasius I, "there are two, O emperor Augustus, by which the world is principally ruled: the sacred authority (*auctoritas*) of pontiffs and the royal power (*potestas*)."[84] This statement is typically taken by modern interpreters to imply the definitive overturning, on the one hand, of "civil religion," that is, the divinizing of the king and sacralizing

of Politics: On the De Regno of Thomas Aquinas (Washington, DC: CUA Press, 2022), 205–54. Where we differ from the argument McCormick offers is that, while McCormick takes the distinction to imply an elimination of any sense of the sacral character of political authority, and so of the sacred from politics simply, we are going to argue, in chapters 2 and 3, that the distinction serves only to clarify the *nature* of the sacred character inherent in politics. The sacred dimension, in other words, is not eliminated but its essence is further specified. It is interesting to note that, after presenting Aquinas's position on the matter, McCormick worries that, even though Aquinas accepts Gelasian dyarchy, he was not sufficiently critical of "theocracy": 211.

84 See the translation of the entire letter, along with commentary, by Pater Edmund Waldstein at https://thejosias.com/2020/03/30/famuli-vestrae-pietatis/.

of civic activities, and, on the other, of "theocracy," that is, the granting of direct political power to religious figures. The statement is thus interpreted as establishing a clear separation of eschatologically-ordered religion from the temporal concerns of the state.[85] While it is true that "dyarchy" is essentially Christian, given that the heart of Christianity is the Incarnation, the hypostatic union of the two radically different natures of God and man formulated at Chalcedon, it is not true that this necessarily implies a clear separation of religion from the temporal order. Until the modern reinterpretation of politics as a reductively pragmatic matter that is no longer concerned with the whole human good, the Church was recognized as being profoundly and intimately involved in temporal human affairs, without this involvement offending against the principle of

85 Compare the radically different view offered by Gerd Tellenbach, who shows that the principle served in profound ways to connect the Church and world more perfectly: *Church, State, and Christian Society at the Time of the Investiture Contest* (New York: Humanities Press, 1970), 33–37.

"dyarchy," but instead being a precise expression of it.[86] Dyarchy is not simply dualism. The Christian king many not have been God, but he was certainly "divine" in the sense of being a privileged human image of God, and being ceremoniously anointed as such. We will offer a theoretical argument in chapters two and three for the sacredness of politics to support this historical fact, but to pursue the argument of the present chapter we wish simply to point out that the claim that the city is the most perfect community because it is ordered to the highest human good to the highest degree is not a denial in principle of "Gelasian dyarchy" but only of its modern interpretation.

86 The question of whether *Dignitatis Humanae*, at Vatican II, has canonized the modern interpretation, which seems to be a dominant assumption among Catholics, cannot be pursued here. We reject this interpretation. For an alternative one, see David L. Schindler and Nicholas J. Healy, *Freedom, Truth, and Human Dignity: The Second Vatican Council's Declaration on Religious Freedom* (Grand Rapids, Mich.: Eerdmans, 2015).

The second objection is that the insistence on the transcendence of the theological reality of the Church betrays the completeness of political community, and the temporal concerns of existence in this world. Rousseau famously held Christianity responsible, precisely by virtue of its introduction of dyarchy, for destroying the possibility of politics in the classical sense and the integrity of the city as it was lived in Greece and Rome, because it appeared to tear man's ultimate allegiance away from the life of this earthly community and direct it to the "afterlife."[87] Rousseau's

---

87 Rousseau, *Social Contract* in *Basic Political Writings* (Indianapolis: Hackett, 1987), 221. See Robert Spaemann, "Natural Existence and Political Existence in Rousseau," in *The Spaemann Reader*, 125–38. Hobbes made a similar claim, though he rejected a separation of ultimate powers in principle and did not lay the blame for this on Christianity; instead, he took the identification of ecclesial and political power in the king to be implied by revelation: see *Leviathan*, esp. part 3 (Oxford: Clarendon Press, 1909), where, for example, 471, he comments on the theory he has presented: "Wherein I pretend not to advance any Position of my own, but

criticism is valid for the modern interpretation of politics, which did indeed radically diminish the scope of the common good, but his solution—namely, to deny any difference between Church and polis and reinstate a new, and indeed purely fabricated, civil religion—reveals that he shared the same dualistic presupposition. We are arguing that a recognition of the transcendence of the Church does not necessarily imply a distraction from the temporal order or a cooling of one's affections for one's city. Rousseau would have been incapable of understanding his later fellow countryman, Charles Péguy, who in one of his poems had God himself wonder if perhaps love of country were even greater than love of God. The point is that, properly understood, self-transcendence in obedience to what lies above coincides with an elevation of nature. Marriage is a proper

onely to shew what are the Consequences that seem to me deducible from the Principles of Christian Politiques, (which are the holy Scriptures,) in confirmation of the Power of Civill Soveralgns, and the Duty of their Subjects."

example in this regard: the "sacramentaliz-ing" of marriage neither transforms it into a religious community nor destroys its imma-nent nature. Instead, in the sacrament, the natural reality of marriage, specifically *as* nat-ural, becomes infinitely more significant as a proper and privileged communication of grace. We will make a similar argument re-garding the political order. The traditional practice of anointing the king was not a re-gressive slip into pagan theocracy, but most basically an affirmation of the full meaning of the natural reality of communal life.

In short, the analogy we are drawing between politics and metaphysics allows us to see how an affirmation of the transcendence of the Church in relation to the temporal realm does not entail a reduction of the scope of poli-tics, but instead radically expands its scope. The political opens up "naturally" to the ecclesial, which transcends it, precisely because political community is ordered to the comprehensive common good. The object that specifies politics in itself is the object that moves it beyond itself to God. This opening up in politics is also es-sentially dramatic, just as it is in metaphysics:

the complete human good cannot *but* include God, who is indeed the "summum bonum," but it cannot include God formally as the human good without further qualification, any more than metaphysics can include God simply within the horizon of (worldly) being.[88] God is the infinitely transcendent origin and end, "Wholly Other" with respect to the world and human being. Because man is by nature ordered to the good as such, he is ordered to God, but this means man is ordered to something that radically transcends his nature. Henri de Lubac's famous formulation of the nature-grace relationship is perfectly fitting to describe this paradox: man has a *natural* desire for a reality that *infinitely surpasses his nature*.[89] This is the

---

88 Ulrich, "Politische Macht," 442.
89 Rudi Te Velde has recently revisited this oft-treated theme, and argued against De Lubac's formulation, in "'Partnership with God': Thomas Aquinas on Human Desire and God's Grace," *Nova et Vetera* 15.4 (2017): 1151–75. But his argument rests on a relentless exclusion of transcendence from nature. As we will argue at greater length in the next chapter, Aquinas is very clear that God is involved in *every single*

"practical" version of the same paradox we witnessed in the theoretical order: God is inevitably *included* within the object of metaphysics but precisely as a cause that lies infinitely beyond that object.

What does all of this mean specifically for God's relationship to the political order? We will be filling out further dimensions of this in our next two chapters, but we can already say, here, in the conclusion of chapter one, that God enters into politics just as indirectly, but just as intrinsically, as he enters into philosophy. God "kommt in" the very essence of both philosophy and politics: He is, we might say, more interior to these orders than they are to themselves, and he is so precisely

human act, elevating it even *as* natural: see *ST* 1.105.3 and 4. Once we see that it is perfectly natural to desire something that in some sense lies beyond nature, even if the very point is to say this is *also* natural (and not a contradiction of nature), then we can affirm De Lubac's formulation. The whole question turns on whether one is capable of grasping genuine paradox, or whether one constantly needs to resolve its complex unity into a multiplicity of separate parts, simpler for the mind to grasp.

because he lies beyond their most transcendent reach. The common good at which the political authority aims is an immanent one, in the sense that it concerns the proper organization of human life on earth, in such a way as to bring that life to its most perfect flourishing possible. As we observed above, the comprehensive good is not comprehensive in a "collective," which is to say a "totalitarian," sense. Though the ruler is concerned with the whole and therefore in some sense even with the lowest of things, this does not mean that he is meant to control all things from top to bottom. Precisely to the contrary: if his thus controlling things is not humanly good, it will be excluded by his being responsible to and for the whole human good. As Plato argued, the power to rule aims *by definition* not at its own perfection, to which it would instrumentalize all below it, but at the perfection of that over which it rules.[90] To take an evident example, the political authority protects the distinct integrity of the family precisely insofar as that authority recognizes as its defining concern

90   Plato, *Republic*, II, 341b-342e.

the *whole* human good. If the integrity of the
family is part of the human good, in other
words, then it is precisely the comprehensiveness of the scope of the political authority that
leads it to respect the integrity of the family.
A political authority that is not defined by
concern for the whole human good will not
have respect for the integrity of the family, except in an accidental way. It is not difficult to
see that the liberal conception of politics in
America that led the Supreme Court to draw
an apparently absolute boundary around the
purely private—i.e., non-political—reality of
marriage and family has not in the least pre-
vented government from intruding into family life in a radical way. This is not a betrayal
of the (purely positively) legal circumscrip-
tion of an absolute sphere of privacy, but its
natural consequence. There is a paradox here,
which is a sign of the Christian "dyarchy": it
is precisely the *inclusion* of specific orders
within the comprehensive political common
good that generates their distinctiveness, and
so allows them to transcend politics.[91]

91   See the earlier note 80.

And something similar can be said for man's relation to God. We have seen that, interpreted as authority, and interpreted in turn as responsible for the *polis*, the ruling power does indeed have a certain responsibility for cultivating man's relationship to God.[92] But this is not his *first* concern; his first concern is the flourishing of man's existence in this world, and he is occupied above all with human excellence.[93] But human excellence is inconceivable without religion, without respect for due worship and man's relation to God. And so the ruler's *comprehensive* authority opens up to an order that transcends the political; we could say that he

92 See R. Jared Staudt, *The Primacy of God: The Virtue of Religion in Catholic Theology* (Steubenville, OH: Emmaus Academic Press, 2022).

93 When Aristotle enumerates the six functions of the political order, and so the responsibilities of the ruler, he mentions religion as fifth, but, apparently correcting himself, adds that it is really *first*: *Politics* VII.8.1328b5-14. We propose that this is not a "slip of the pen," but in fact gives subtle expression to the way God enters into politics: not as a defining object, but nevertheless as fundamental to every defining object.

is responsible for ensuring that the political order is always more than political,[94] which is to say that he is responsible for ensuring that our existence in the City of Man be as far as possible a mode of living in the City of God. Aquinas's succinct formulation in the *De Regno* of the ruler's responsibility captures both dimensions, God's transcendence of the political common good and his immanence within it. It is *because* the ruler is responsible for the whole human good, the "highest good to the highest degree," that his office requires him to foster human excellence, that is, completeness or perfection, in such a way that it naturally opens beyond itself: "since society must have the same end as the individual man, it is not the ultimate end of an assembled multitude to live virtuously, but through virtuous living to attain to the possession of God."[95]

To conclude this chapter, it is worth indicating how strikingly different this point is from the regnant liberal conception of the

94   See *ST* 1-2.21.4ad3.
95   Aquinas, *De Regno*, I.15 [109].

"separation of Church and State." Liberals tend to think that we best ensure the integrity of religion by insisting on the state's incompetence in such matters. But we have argued that political rule *cannot but* represent the whole human good in some respect, and this means it cannot but, by implication, communicate a distinctive conception of God and institutionalize the proper relation to God so conceived. If this is true, it is precisely a liberal conception of the state that will be totalitarian, insofar as it will inevitably institutionalize what constitutes legally sanctioned religious practice, but now in complete indifference to the Church, which is to say in indifference to any authority higher than itself.[96] By thus policing religious practice, it becomes the supreme authority that trumps all others, perhaps not in the secret heart of individuals, but nevertheless in the sphere

96 For a longer argument on this point, based on the metaphysical principle that a whole is prior to its parts and actuality is prior to potency, see my "The Merely Political Common Good: On the Totalitarianism of Incompetence," *Politics of the Real*, 69–105.

that everyone is required to recognize. In other words, the state becomes the supreme power *in reality*. And this assumption of supreme power does not have to justify itself because it does not make any explicit claims in this regard; it simply seizes supreme power *de facto*, in a manner that does not permit any challenge or acknowledge any contenders. As the great twentieth-century political philosophers Hannah Arendt and Augusto del Noce have argued, the only way finally to avoid totalitarianism is by recovering genuine authority.[97] Or we can say it is only through a recognition of the ruling power's responsibility to and for the whole human good—the highest good to the highest degree in the most perfect sense—that allows God to enter into politics . . . and remain God.

97 Hannah Arendt, "What is Authority?," in *Between Past and Future* (New York: Penguin, 2006), 110, and Augusto del Noce, "Authority versus Power," *The Crisis of Modernity* (Montreal: McGill-Queen's University Press, 2014), 206.

Chapter Two
The City Is the Soul
Writ Large:
On God as a *Res Publica*

If God does indeed "enter politics," as we have just argued, he does so in and through man, the subject of political community. God is present to each and every individual human person by nature, but he is present in a distinctive way to man specifically *in community*. While most people might acknowledge some aspect of the social character of the relation to God when it comes to religious congregations, it is crucial to see that this point also bears inevitably on the natural political order. In the current chapter, we will advance some reason to think that if we fail to recognize the essentially political dimension of relation to God, we will be unable properly to grasp the presence of God in the (ecclesial and sacramental) Body of Christ: God cannot be real in the Church *as* Church unless he is also real in the city *as* city (and vice versa).[98] Relation to God, realized most properly in faith, has an essentially social, or corporate, dimension.[99]

In order to make this case, we must first deepen our sense of the "connection" between man and the polis, or in other words between human nature and community in

98 To respond straightaway to an immediate objection on this score, which would point to the thriving of the Church especially in times of persecution, that is, when the Church was violently excluded from the public sphere, we would say that one affirms the essentially corporate dimension of faith implicitly precisely by recognizing this exclusion as persecution: violence is being done not just to the individual with respect to his "private" convictions, but specifically to the truth and the reality of the faith, which demands a corporate realization: both a corporate recognition and a corporate *life*.

99 See the classic text on this point, Henri de Lubac, *Catholicism: Christ and the Common Destiny of Man* (San Francisco: Ignatius, 1988).

the good. This connection has been a theme in classical philosophy from the beginning. Its best-known expression occurs no doubt in book II of the *Republic*, which opens the discussion of justice from the virtue of an individual's existence to its properly political dimensions. If we wish to understand the significance of justice in the human soul, Socrates says, we need to view it projected, so to speak, on a larger screen, investigating how this virtue is realized in the organized inter-relation between individuals (and classes of individuals) in community.[100] As the famous formulation puts it, Plato's move from the individual to the community is justified because the "city is the soul writ large." What does this mean? What exactly is the relationship between the order of the soul and the order of the city, between human nature and politics?

Aristotle speaks directly to this question in his claim that the end of man and the end of the city are one and the same, a claim that

100 Plato, *Republic*, II, 368c-369b.

Aquinas echoes.[101] Let us think about what this means more concretely. One way to interpret the claim is to read it abstractly, or in other words in a purely formal sense. In this case, it means that there is an identity of content between the two, such that, whatever specific goods are contained in the one are contained in the other, even if they are realized differently in the two contexts[102]: happiness is the end of each individual man, so happiness is also the purpose of common life; happiness requires virtue, so virtue is the end of each individual man, and also the purpose of common life. And so on.[103] While

---

101 Aristotle, *Politics*, VII.2.1324a5-13; Aquinas, *De Regno*, I.15 [107]; cf., *Commentary on the Politics*, V.3 [387].

102 Aquinas points to a formal difference in the realization of goodness in the individual and in the community: *ST* 2-2.58.7ad2. We ought to say that there is a difference of analogy, and not just quantity, between these orders, which is why they do not enter into competition with each other in principle.

103 Aristotle himself seems to approach the matter in this way, at least on the surface: "For those who hold that the well-being of the individual

this formal identity is certainly true, however much it may be denied in modern political philosophy,[104] we propose to interpret the claim here in a more robust and concretely material sense: the good around which the community gathers itself so as to be truly a community—in other words, the political common good—is the good that man as such desires. Even more specifically, man desires not only a particular good, or indeed an ordered set of goods, which corresponds to his nature, he desires to possess these goods specifically in the mode of sharing them with others.[105]

consists in his wealth also think that riches make the happiness of the whole state." He of course disagrees with this judgment, and ultimately shows that *virtue* is the proper end, but he does not appear to disagree with the *type* of answer given to the question.

104 Modern politics can in fact be defined as having severed the connection.

105 To be sure, Aquinas says explicitly that "the fellowship of friends is not essential to Happiness," in the sense of ultimate beatitude: *ST* 1-2.4.8. De Koninck properly qualifies Aquinas's claim by saying that the good loved

In other words, man desires to possess his good, no matter what kind of good it may be, precisely in a participatory way. We mean by this claim to go beyond the traditional expression of man's social nature in the affirmation that man naturally loves the good of the whole *more* than his individual good[106]; while this is true, we propose to radicalize it in two respects: first, by pointing out that, while the "more" here can on occasion mean that he desires to sacrifice his individual good in order to affirm the greater good, it has a more profound, and universal, sense, namely, that one naturally loves the common, or transcendent, dimension of the good more than the particular and individual-related dimension of the good *in every single good one loves*, whether that good be one that belongs to oneself or belongs to the larger

in this case remains essentially *communicable by nature*, even if not actually *communicated*, but we ought to press the point further, as we mean to do in this chapter.

106 Aquinas, *ST* 1.60.corpus, ad1 and ad3.

community.[107] This is an implication of Aquinas's claim that the good as such moves us in every act of appetite, and that we know and love God, the most universal good, in every act of knowledge and will.[108] Second, this implies that the particular good that I love stands out as all the more good and all the more loveable the more I perceive it as somehow a part of the community, or as contributing to the community in some way. Aquinas explains that a good can be both particular and common in this respect.[109]

---

107 Aquinas in fact says that the common good belongs to each individual (*ST* 2-2.58.9ad3), and explains that "a man's will is not right in willing a particular good, unless he refer it to the common good as an end: since even the natural appetite of each part is ordained to the common good of the whole" (ST 1-2.19.10).

108 *De ver.*, 22.2; *ST* 1-2.8.1, and 1-2.9.6.

109 ST 2-2.58.5: "whatever is the good of a part can be directed to the good of the whole." In ST 1-2.90.2ad2, he writes that "it is clear that good has the nature of an end; wherefore, a particular end of anything consists in some particular good; while the universal end of all things is the Universal Good; Which is good of Itself by

Man is so radically social that the reference to the larger community in the particular good that he loves intensifies the delight that it gives him even as an individual; this is why, Aquinas observes, the pleasure of sex (which refers to the species) is more intense than the pleasure of eating, which, at least at one level, concerns the individual alone.[110]

Let us illustrate how the good the individual loves deepens when it is affirmed in a participatory way. According to the classical tradition, stemming from Aristotle,

---

virtue of Its Essence, Which is the very essence of goodness; whereas a particular good is good by participation. Now it is manifest that in the whole created universe there is not a good which is not such by participation."

110 "Now pleasures are proportionate to the actions whose perfections they are, as stated in Ethic. ix, 4,5: and it is evident that actions connected with the use of food whereby the nature of the individual is maintained differ generically from actions connected with the use of matters venereal, whereby the nature of the species is preserved": ST 2-2.151.3; cf., ST 2-2.151.2ad2 and 3ad2.

man is a rational animal and he is a political animal. As an animal, man desires food. Typically, food is identified as a particular good, because, in contrast to the properly common good of, say, truth, it cannot be shared without being diminished.[111] Physical goods, related to our animal nature, divide us in a basic way; they must be distributed severally.[112] For one individual to eat something is to consume it and so to take away the possibility that another individual has of eating that thing: What I put in my mouth nourishes me alone. But human beings are not merely animals; we are *rational* and *political* animals. This quality is not simply superadded to our animal nature, layered on top of a baser, and more basic, foundation, but penetrates into our animal nature so to speak and informs it

111 See, for example, Reginald Garrigou-Lagrange, *Life Everlasting and the Immensity of the Soul* (Charlotte, NC: TAN Books, 1991), part I, §3.
112 See Gregory Froelich on the "bona communia," which is distinct from the bonum commune: "The Ambiguity of 'Common Good'," reprinted in *New Polity* 2.2 (2021): 33–42, here: 40–41.

from top to bottom.[113] *Everything* we do, without exception, to the extent that it is an *actus humanus*, we do as both an animal and a rational/political being, and indeed the rational/political dimension is always the

113 "For, although the sensitive souls in man and brute are generically alike, they differ specifically, as do the things whose forms they are; since, just as the human animal differs specifically from the other animals by the fact that it is rational, so the sensitive soul of man differs specifically from the sensitive soul of the brute by the fact that it is also intellective. Therefore, in the soul of the brute there is nothing suprasensitive, and, consequently, it transcends the body neither in being nor in operation; and that is why the brute soul must be generated together with the body and perish with the body. But in man the sensitive soul is possessed of intellective power over and above the sensitive nature and is therefore raised above the body both in being and in operation": Aquinas, SCG 2.89.12 (I owe this reference to Marc Barnes). Note that it is the *sensitive soul* that is possessed of intellective power, and not simply that the intellective power is an additional power added to that of the sensitive soul. In other words, the transcendence of the spiritual soul permeates the whole of the human being.

decisive one, even in what might be considered our more animal concerns. The specifically *human* desire for food, for example, is not simply a desire to ingest fuel for physical survival; it is a desire for a shared meal, wherein the physical and the cultural, the material and the spiritual, the individual and the social elements are inseparably intertwined.[114] It is only in such a properly formed, communal context that our physical desire to eat is properly satisfied—which is no doubt one of the reasons why a culture that has lost social forms tends to face the problem of widespread obesity. Man is rational and political "all the way down," just as he is animal "all the way up."

Something of this social elevation and transformation of the human good is indicated in Aristotle's well-known claim that the city initially came into being for the sake of mere survival (*zēn, vivere*: to live), but it

114 For a fascinating study of the complex act of human eating in all of its dimensions, see Margaret Visser, *The Rituals of Dinner* (New York: Penguin, 1992).

exists for the sake of well-being (*eu zēn, bene vivere*), or in other words, well-being defines the essence of the human community.[115] The distinctively human good, which passes through the mediation of human freedom and intelligence, or in other words human culture, can be properly possessed only as given and received in community with others. Aquinas points in this direction by extending the exercise of one's own natural powers to include the acts of those to whom

---

115 There is a more profound ontological point being made here than is generally realized, which concerns in fact the nature of coming-to-be simply: the essence of a substance can never be reductively accounted for by the set of material conditions in which it has arisen; there is always what we might call a "from-above" aspect, which necessarily accompanies the simplicity of form. What was most novel in the Darwinian interpretation of evolution was not so much the idea of change over time, but the elimination of this basic distinction. This is a metaphysical, and indeed ultimately theological move, and not a "scientific" one. On all of this, see Robert Spaemann, "Being and Coming-to-Be: What Does the Theory of Evolution Explain?", *The Robert Spaemann Reader*, 154–69.

one is bound in friendship (which, we might point out, ultimately implies that happiness has the form of a gift).[116] But Augustine makes the point quite explicit: the common good that we aim at cannot be possessed *except* as shared,[117] and all goods that we desire are analogously forms of peace, which is a harmonious unity of many gathered into one.[118] The shared character of this good is so essential to human desire, we must affirm that political community is itself a good sought, or in other words, it is an intrinsic

116 Aquinas, *ST*, 1-2.5.5ad2; cf., also ST 1-2.91.4ad3 and 109.4ad2; *De ver.*, 8.3ad12, 24.10ad1; and *De malo*, 5.1. In a recent text, John Milbank illustrates this point by referencing the act of sexual intercourse, for which man has a natural desire, but at the same time it is one that requires the free gift of another person for its proper fulfillment: see "Catholic Social Teaching as Political Theology," in *New Polity* 3.2 (Spring 2022): 26..

117 Augustine, *On Christian Doctrine*, I.1: "For a possession which is not diminished by being shared with others, if it is possessed and not shared, is not yet possessed as it ought to be possessed."

118 Augustine, *City of God*, XIX.12 and 13; cf., *City of God*, XV.5.

and not merely instrumental good of human nature.[119] We form community not just to be able to achieve certain goods impossible otherwise, but because it belongs to the highest human good to *be* in community. The republic is itself a *res publica*, which is to say the city is itself part of the common good that is cultivated by the people who constitute it.[120]

119 Robert George, by contrast, argues that political community "is primarily a means to the realization of valuable ends by members of the community; it is not an end in itself": "The Common Good: Instrumental But Not Just Contractual," *thepublicdiscourse*.com/2013/05/10166/. In this, he departs from the classical vision of human nature and its relation to the political order. For a very sophisticated and nuanced account of the political common good, see Gregory Froelich, "The Ambiguity of 'Common Good." Froelich's account of the "bonum in praedicando" would have to be qualified by a metaphysics that is more appreciative of the Neoplatonic tradition, one able to affirm a certain ontological, and therefore causal, status of universals even while rejecting their "real" existence as such.

120 According to Aristotle, "one citizen differs from another, but the salvation of the community is the common business of them all," *Politics*,

If man is a *political* animal, this does not only mean that he is inherently *social*—i.e., naturally inclined to form relations with others. Instead, it means that each individual man's natural desire for fulfillment comes to a certain rest in the polis, the organized community of a city. The end of man and the end of the city are one and the same, which is one of the reasons the city is the soul writ large.[121]

We wish to argue that this point bears on the manner in which God enters the political sphere. In the previous chapter, we pointed to the analogy of sacramental marriage as a way of showing how God, and the life of worship, can enter into a natural community

---

III.4.1276b27-29. Also, see the texts from Aquinas cited in Froelich, "The Ambiguity of the Common Good," fn. 39, which explain that "justice, as the civil order of the community, is itself a common good *per modum causae*": ST 1-2.19.10, ST 1-2.96.3, ST 2-2.33.6, and *In Ethic.*, lect. 6, n. 1839.

121 This affirmation does not exclude the radical difference of analogy; it is not the case, in other words, that the order of the soul simply "lines up" with the order of the city in a simple one-to-one correspondence.

from the inside (but never *only* from the inside) without making that community any less natural or intruding on and displacing its naturally given form and ends. What we intend to do in the present chapter is develop a further dimension of this analogy. God, and indeed *the Church*, can enter sacramentally into a marriage only if the two spouses are baptized, which is to say only if they already have been elevated into the sacramental economy of grace. But God's, and indeed the Church's, effective presence inside the marriage is not simply a presence to each one individually, or simply to their sum. Instead, through sacramental grace, the marriage *itself* is able to become, so to speak, the "holy place" wherein the individuals live their relation to God. Their household in this way becomes an *ecclesiola* or an *ecclesia domestica*, which means both that certain liturgical practices can be naturally part of domestic life and, more profoundly, that the natural activities of marriage and family themselves give glory to God and become means of grace. In short, the marriage itself comes to be the proper "locus" of the holiness of the spouses, in a manner analogous to the way in which the monastic community is the "locus" of the holiness of the monks.[122] It is not just that the family, with its usual challenges, provides unique occasions for individuals to pursue virtue and perfect spiritual practices. Instead, the family is itself a place wherein one's relation to God becomes *real*.

In light of the point we made earlier, we may say that this rich reality of marriage, which has not only a cultural dimension but also a political and ecclesial dimension, is the properly human fulfillment of the animal desire for reproduction. By analogy, we will argue below that man's natural desire for God, because it is human, seeks fulfillment in a communal reality, as a publicly-constituted *res*. The city is not a sacramental reality in the strict sense, in which we participate through baptism—even if the medieval city, ultimately under the authority of a sacramentally anointed king, in which one received citizenship through baptism, certainly

122 See David Crawford, *Marriage and the Sequela Christi* (Rome: Lateran, 2004).

suggests something of the sort.[123] Nevertheless, precisely because it represents the ordering of human existence to the highest good in the highest respect (an ordering that makes the common good something "divine"[124]), and because this good is inseparable from God, the city presents a realization of the relation to God that is analogous to that found in marriage.[125] Man's relation to God does not begin, after all, only with baptism, but is, so to speak, already there in his innermost nature (even if baptism is a

---

123 See the account in Augustine Thompson, O.P., *Cities of God: The Religion of the Italian Communes 1125-1325* (University Park: Penn State University Press, 2005), 311–14.

124 Aquinas, ST 2-2.99.1ad1.

125 Analogy of course means both similarity and difference. We cannot lay out the details here, but one might present the community of the Church, which *is* sacramental in the strict sense, and the community of the *polis*, which is not sacramental, but, by virtue of its intrinsic relation to the Church, something "quasi-sacramental," as representing the two-fold aspect of marriage (and indeed the two natures of Christ).

re-birth, a recapitulation of this "natural" relation from its roots in the new order), and
so his desire for God inevitably seeks fulfillment in the natural reality of his common
life, precisely *as* common.

We will seek to show this by exploring in
more depth the precise way in which God is
present to man by nature: God is present to
the essence of man, God is present in man's
end, and God is present in all of man's operations, which is to say that God is inevitably
"part" of human life in the order of formal,
final, and efficient causality. Because a good
deal has been written about the first two aspects, we will be fairly brief on those points,
focusing most attention on the last, which is
especially relevant here given that the political order is essentially practical, the sphere
of action. We will then explore the implications of this presence of God specifically in
the human activity of ruling, and, finally,
consider what this entails with respect to
man's natural aptitude for community: the
desire for God that is rooted in, and so gives
form to, man's *nature*, is rooted in and gives
form specifically to man's *political* nature.

Regarding the first point, it is altogether uncontroversial, at least from the perspective of the classical Christian tradition, to affirm that God is present *in* creation, however little attention might be given to the implications of this fact in certain contexts. God is not present in a vague or general way, but exists, as Aquinas puts it, in all things—that is, in each one individually and in all altogether—by "essence, presence, and power."[126] Indeed, it is crucial to note that God is not simply present *to* things as a reality standing over against them, but, while this is also true, God is always-already present *in* things "innermostly" (*intime*). This means that relation to God is not something the creature establishes in its operations, but is always antecedently presupposed in some sense in every operation, because the very being of all things is receptive to God by virtue of the act of creation.[127] In this respect, it is proper to say that all creatures are constitutively related to God. If this is true generally, it is

126 Aquinas, *ST* 1.8.3.
127 Aquinas, *ST*, 1.45.3.

especially true of man, who is, uniquely among corporeal creatures, not a *trace* but an *image* of God.[128] To call man "imago" means that man analogously resembles God, but even more fundamentally, as we will see below, that man is intimately related to God.

Regarding the second point, there has been, and perhaps always in some sense will be, much controversy, specifically in the great "nature-grace" debate that took place among Catholic theologians particularly in the twentieth century. The principal controversy turns on the question, What place does the Trinitarian God revealed in Jesus Christ have in man's natural desire for fulfillment? But while responding to that question and resolving the controversy would be essential to the development of an adequate political theology, the question that is more immediate to our present inquiry, sketching the principles of what I propose to call a "political metaphysics," is the far less controversial question, What place does God, as *principium et finis* of creation, have in

128 Aquinas, *ST* 1.93.1, 2, and 6.

man's desire? The classical Christian tradition has generally recognized that, because of his spiritual nature, which means because man is ordered to being, goodness, and truth in its absolute and unrestricted sense, man cannot find fulfillment specifically *as* man except in God. Note that this means even temporal happiness is an enjoyment of God in a manner analogous to final beatitude. In other words, if there is a distinction, as there surely is, between earthly happiness and perfect eschatological fulfillment, God bridges the distinction, insofar as he is relevant to both sides. Because God infinitely transcends the world, and thus the realm of nature as a whole, it is proper to say that man has a natural desire for a supernatural end, even if there remains an ambiguity in the meaning of the word "supernatural" here—whether it means God simply as transcending the created order (which is a truth accessible to natural reason as such, and found, for example, very clearly in a figure such as Plotinus, apparently independently of Christian revelation) or it means God as revealed in Jesus Christ and effective specifically in the order of grace and redemption.

We would like to propose that the human desire for happiness presents the same sort of dramatic reversal and fulfillment that, as we saw in the last chapter, can be found in what Aquinas designates as the highest realization of the human spirit in the theoretical and practical order, respectively: namely, metaphysics and politics. In the first, metaphysics, man pursues as complete an understanding as possible of the highest object of the intellect, being, in its essential qualities and ultimate causes, and this opens him up naturally to the God who is beyond nature because he transcends created being.[129] In the second, politics, man pursues "the highest good to the highest degree," that is, the ultimate end as possessed in common, and this naturally opens him up to the God that transcends the horizon of this world.[130]

---

129 Aquinas, *Commentary on the Metaphysics*, prologue.
130 See Aquinas, *De Regno*, I.15 [106 and 107]; cf., *Commentary on the Nichomachean Ethics*, II.2 [30].

The Thomistic tradition, of course, commonly affirms that man has a twofold end, natural happiness and supernatural beatitude. Affirming this truth in principle, we must nevertheless avoid thinking of God as lying so to speak exclusively on the "supernatural" side of happiness.[131] Because man is a spiritual being *by nature*, and not just *by grace*, and because spirit is essentially ordered to being, truth, and goodness in their unrestricted senses, God is essentially "part" of man's happiness even in "this" world. To say it again, man has a natural desire for an end that infinitely transcends man, which is to say that man's desire for happiness even in this life and within the horizon of the temporal order, is implicitly, and inescapably, a desire for God. What Aquinas refers to as "imperfect" earthly happiness, distinct from supernatural beatitude, in other words, is itself even as earthly wholly ordered in

---

131 For a longer argument, see my essay, "Integralism as Fragmentation: A Response to Pater Edmund Waldstein," *New Polity* 2.2 (May 2021): 21–32.

relation to God to the extent that it is in any meaningful sense at all *human* happiness.

This last observation leads us to the third point mentioned above, which is that God is present to man in the order of efficient causality. As we remarked initially, this aspect of the theme does not seem to have drawn as much attention, except in some of the more abstract discussions of free will and divine providence or pre-destination. In question 105, articles 3 and 4, in his treatise on divine government in the *pars prima* of the *Summa*,[132] Aquinas raises the question whether God moves the created intellect and will immediately, which is to say whether God is involved directly in properly human action. His answer is an unqualified yes, and he explains this involvement in a far more comprehensive way than one might think. God is present not only as the ultimate object of our

---

132 It is worth noting that God's involvement in the actual ordering of the cosmos is presented under the name "government" (*gubernatione*), which of course evokes the analogy with human rule that we are elaborating in this book.

intellect and will, he says, but also on the subjective end, so to speak, as the ultimate Agent of these acts.

Let us take these two acts, that of the intellect and that of the will, sequentially. First of all, God is so to speak constitutively present to the human intellect insofar as the intellect is what it is by participation in the divine intellect, so much so that we must affirm that God creates each individual human soul immediately.[133] More specifically, in each act of understanding, God is immediately present implicitly in the object of understanding as its source and exemplar cause (the form of its form, as it were), and therefore is the actual cause of that form's intelligibility.[134] He is at the same time present as the moving principle of the intellect: "The intellectual operation is performed by the intellect in which it exists [that is, by the

133 Aquinas, *ST* 1.90.2.
134 Note that this claim avoids the error of ontologism because it insists that God is present implicitly and indirectly, in an analogous rather than univocal manner. God is not directly intuited in this life.

individual human knower], as by a secondary cause; but it proceeds from God as from its first cause."[135] In a manner reminiscent of Plato's claim in the *Republic* that the idea of the Good gives truth to the thing known and the power to know to the knower,[136] Aquinas affirms that God unites the knower and known by being both the present source of their existence and also the actual cause of the operation by which they come together, causing the union so to speak on both sides at once. Let us note that this involvement of God in man's understanding concerns every single operation, no matter what the object may be, not just those explicitly directed to theological matters.

In like fashion, Aquinas explains in article 4 that God moves every single act of will, also from both sides. God is first of all himself alone the universal good at which the will inevitably aims by definition, since the will is the appetite in its intellectual mode, i.e., as ordered to the good specifically in its

135 Aquinas, *ST* 1.105.3ad1.
136 Plato, *Republic*, 508e-509a.

unrestricted sense.[137] But God moves the will not only "extrinsically" by being the ultimate attraction, so to speak, which sets the will in operation. *Even more fundamentally*, Aquinas says, God moves the will interiorly, by disposing the will to himself. The argument here is a crucial one:

> God alone is the universal good. Whereas He alone fills the capacity of the will, and moves it sufficiently as its object. In like manner, the power of willing is caused by God alone. For to will is nothing but to be inclined towards the object of the will, which is universal good. But to incline towards the universal good belongs to the First Mover, to Whom the ultimate end is proportionate; just as in human affairs to him that presides over the community belongs the directing of his subjects to the common weal [*ad bonum*

137 Cf., Aquinas, *ST* 1-2.8.1.

commune]. Wherefore in both ways it belongs to God to move the will, but especially [*maxime*] in the second way by an interior inclination of the will.[138]

At the core of this argument is the classic Greek insight that a potency can be reduced to act only by something already in a state of actuality, which implies that no object can move an appetite without already being in some sense effectively present in the appetite already at the outset.[139] The final cause is necessarily the first cause, the cause of all other causes, and, as Heidegger never tired of repeating, what shows itself at the end brings to light what has been present from the most original beginning. To use more scholastic language to make the same point, the *end* of a motion is its *principium*, a meaningful motion ultimately comes to rest in its point of departure. One of the reasons this point is so

---

138 Aquinas, *ST* 1.105.4.
139 This is one of the basic themes of my book *Retrieving Freedom* (Notre Dame, IN: University of Notre Dame Press, 2022).

important is that it sheds a light on the na-ture-grace debate mentioned above that is not often recognized. As Aquinas points out here, it is not only the pursuit of man's su-pernatural end that exceeds man's nature and so requires God's assistance in the form of grace; it is also the case that the very object that *defines* man's will, and so constitutes its innermost and essential nature, namely, the universal good, exceeds that nature by virtue of its universality, which in some respect is disproportionate to his individuality.[140] This does not make the willing of the good a su-pernatural act in the strict sense, i.e., in the sense that would oppose it to nature (as some interpret Augustine to have affirmed); in other words, God does not move the will

140 Notice that this is a disproportionality within the same natural order, which is why this excess is a natural analogue to the more radical excess of grace, the supernatural in the strict sense. We pointed out above Rudi Te Velde's failure to grasp this point, which is why he is not able to make sense of de Lubac's statement that man has a natural desire for the supernatural (see his "Partnership with God").

in spite of itself and its natural capacities. Instead, the will has a natural capacity for the good, but that natural capacity is inconceivable without the actual assistance of God.

Note, it is not just that God must actively dispose man whenever man wills *God* directly. God's actual disposition of the will is altogether universal: there is no act of the human will that is not rooted in, and activated by, God. As intellectual appetite, the will moves itself to any and all of its objects by being, implicitly or explicitly, moved by goodness *per se*, which is to say, moved by God. If the will is an intellectual appetite, it cannot move itself in any act at all without that act being caused immediately by God, both as end and as principal efficient agent. This point, perhaps more than any other, brings home the reality of the presence of God in *all* of man's activities, most fully of course in those activities that directly concern ultimate ends and the meaning of life, but even unto the least of things, to the extent that these are human. It is indeed the case that it is only in God that "we live and move and have our being," and this is a matter of our nature, even in its fallen condition.[141] It is impossible to conceive of human existence outside of this comprehensive and liberating presence of God without falling into incoherence. While the all-embracing actual and active presence of God is a universal truth relevant to all being all the time, it concerns man in a paradigmatic way because of his spiritual nature. The *animal rationale* is inescapably *homo religiosus*.

But if this is true for the *rational animal*, it is especially true, and true in a distinctive way, for the *political animal*. Given Aquinas's explanation of the operation of the human intellect and will, we can infer that God's presence in human action will be fuller, and more manifest, the more that action concerns the good as such, explicitly and directly, and so in its analogously universal mode. It is illuminating to consider the nature of political authority specifically in the light of this inference. In the *De Regno*, Aquinas argues for the need for a ruling power on the basis of

141 Acts 17;28; St. Paul is quoting the Greek poet Epimenides.

the relation that holds between means and ends in human action: because man is a rational and free creature, this relation is not naturally given, but requires determination, which is why a distinct principle is required to deliberate and choose the best means available. For an individual with respect to his own acts, this principle is *reason*, which is like a king, Aquinas says, in the individual soul.[142] A multiplicity of individuals requires that the principle be embodied in an actual authority, distinct from the individuals in their multiplicity, in order to coordinate this activity; the authority has the charge of directing the acts in consort to the good that unites them. Because there is a natural tendency for individuals to act in relation to their proper good, there is a need for an individual to be set apart and given the distinct duty, the *office* [*officium*], of care for the common good precisely *as* common. Note that we have here yet another instance of an external "help" needed for what is natural—namely, the desire for the common good—to

142 Aquinas, *De Regno*, I.1 [4].

find its proper realization. We have just seen that God is present in all human action to the extent that it aims at the good, which means that it refers to a principle that transcends its immediate relation to the particulars of the situation in which the action occurs. Now, in the *De Regno*, we find that, in a community, there must be a ruling power that is *charged specifically with this concern*, that is, with looking to the common good as such beyond the individuals in the particular pursuits proper to them. The difference between the individual members of a city and the ruling power that represents the city that makes them a community is not simply a difference of degree. Instead, it is "official"; it has an institutionalized character. The ruler is publicly recognized as having the duty of caring for the common good. But if the ruler's acts are specifically ordered to the common good, it means that the relation to God, which belongs in general to all human activity, belongs in an analogously "official" way to the ruling power. God is not only implicitly present in the ruler's activity as he is in all of our ordinary human acts; he becomes publicly, *officially*, present, precisely insofar as the political authority is occupied with the human good *simpliciter*. God is present in the acts of state, so to speak, even more directly than in the acts of man, even though of course God is universally present throughout.

St. Paul affirmed that "There is no authority (ἐξουσία) except from God, and those that exist have been instituted (τεταγμένα) by God" (Rom 13:1). This affirmation has been a central one for the Christian interpretation of politics throughout the tradition.[143] Aquinas affirms it himself in various places. Often, one takes the claim in a rather superficial sense, namely, that the authority possessed by those in power can ultimately be traced back in origin to God, and so by obeying earthly rulers we by implication are obeying God. This superficial reading is reflected in the theory of "divine right of kings," which affirms the simple *fact* of ruling power having its origins in God but

---

143 See Emilie Tardivel, *Tout pouvoir vient de Dieu* (Paris: Ad Solem, 2015), for an exposition of the use of this phrase among the Fathers.

without properly recognizing that this origin bears essentially on the *form* of power and so on the manner of its exercise. For a revealing illustration, consider Bertrand de Jouvenel's observations on the natural contextualization of the royal power in the medieval period when the king was anointed by the pope and was thereby inserted into a greater order that relativizes his might. It was the loss of this connection between the Church and the kingdom in the rise of the "divine right of kings" that allowed regal power to conceive itself in absolute terms.[144] We propose a more ontological, and in some sense sacramental, interpretation of the derivation of regal power from God, based on our reflections up to this point. In other words, we would like to suggest that political authority is something like a natural sacrament, radically different, to be sure, from the seven sacraments in the strict, theological, sense, but nevertheless bearing some analogy to

144 Bertrand de Jouvenel, *On Power: The Natural History of Its Growth* (New York: Viking Penguin, 1976), 30-35.

them insofar as it represents a privileged way of communicating the presence of God.[145] First of all, we see that St. Paul's statement has a universal scope; it refers not only to political authority but to all authority, or indeed all power, simply. Read in relation to our foregoing argument, it brings to light the very being of human action: as ordered to the good, it involves God in an intimate way, in terms of form, finality, and efficiency. This

---

145 See Aquinas, *ST* 2-2.99.1ad1. This was a common view in the Middle Ages. Consider, for example, the fact that, in proposing a new theory of signs, Peter Olivi sets aside two special cases wherein God acts directly, namely, in the sacraments and in political authority: Ferdinand Delorme, "Question de P.J. Olivi, 'Quid ponant ius vel dominium,' ou encore, 'De signis voluntaris,'" in *Antonianum* 20 (1945): 309–30, cited in Giorgio Agamben, *The Highest Poverty* (Stanford: Stanford University Press, 2013), 136. Gerd Tellenbach, somewhat misleadingly, refers to this phenomenon as "royal theocracy," meaning to distinguish this participation of the king in the sacred order from "theocracy" in the more usual sense, i.e., a priest's taking over temporal government: *Church, State, and Christian Society* (New York: Humanities Press, 1970), 56–60.

ontological involvement allows us to see
that, if God is involved in a *special* way in political authority, as he is indeed, it is not simply by giving a divine sanction to an
otherwise purely human activity; instead,
God is *intrinsically present* in political authority in a manner that, given the argument
made above, we can call "quasi-sacramental." In carrying out his office, and so making
the common good effectively present by ordering human activity to that good, the ruling power communicates God to the city in
a distinctive way. We mentioned at the outset
Aquinas's observation that the common
good that sets the political horizon is the
highest good to the highest degree, which
therefore opens up intrinsically to God. We
now see the complementary point, namely,
that the political authority that cares for the
common good in an official way derives
from and reflects God. It is only when we affirm the latter that we can properly understand and affirm the former, and vice versa.
As we noted above, all motion begins from
its end; a motion to the common good, which
opens to God, must itself begin from God,

the unrestricted perfection of goodness. The common good, Aquinas says, as the highest actual form of goodness, is divine, and therefore so must be—in an ontological sense and not simply in appearance—the authority appointed to pursue it.[146]

Political authority has *always,* throughout history, had a divine aura, so to speak. While we typically think that this is true only in pre-Christian, or at least pre-modern cultures, it is not difficult to see that this judgment is superficial, and in fact dangerously so. Christianity certainly radicalized the distinction between the eschaton and the immanenton, so to speak, but the Church also anointed her kings, ritually introducing them into what some theologians took to be holy orders,[147] though the precise nature of

146 Aquinas refers to political authority as sacred in a sense that is analogical to the sacraments (*per quandam nominis extensionem*) because the common good is "*quoddam divinum*": see, again, *ST*, 2-2.99.1ad1.

147 According to Tellenbach, "The Church took account of [the ruler's sacred character] in the ceremony of royal consecration, which was

the king's ecclesial status was not clarified until Popes Innocent III and John XII distinguished the anointing of the king from priestly ordination at the beginning of the thirteenth century.[148] As the organic unity between the Church and the Christian kingdom—the unity of Christendom—faded at the dawn of modernity, political authority did not in fact become less religious; it is just that the nature of its religiousness changed.[149] The "divine right of kings," after

reckoned among the sacraments in the early middle ages, and so drew kingship into its spiritual territory. In the ceremony of consecration, it was held, God gave the king something of His power through His servants the bishops, and as a result the king became 'a new man.' At his anointing the emperor was, as an expression of this inner change, received into the ranks of the clergy," *Church, State, and Christian Society*, 57.

148 See Francis Oakley, *The Mortgage of the Past* (New Haven: Yale University Press, 2012), 163.

149 John Sommerville insightfully characterizes one aspect of this change as a shift from "religious culture" to "religious faith": *The Secularization of Early Modern England* (Oxford: Oxford University Press, 1992).

all, is a modern theory. The governments after the Reformation became even more explicitly and deliberately religious, in some sense, than the medieval forms before it.[150] The French Revolution, which was a radical break from the previous Christian tradition, though it overthrew the Church, quite explicitly installed a new god, presumably because political authority is inconceivable except as rooted in the divine.[151] For a time, there were some who believed that the American Founders were finally able to achieve what the Christian tradition could not, namely, a *truly neutral* conception of political authority, which allows religion finally to purify itself of any relation to the institutional structures of the world. But it has become compellingly clear, both theoretically *and* phenomenologically—in light of the ersatz religious meaning spontaneously given

150 See Eric Nelson, *The Hebrew Republic: Jewish Sources and the Transformation of European Political Thought* (Cambridge, MA: Harvard University Press, 2011).

151 Hannah Arendt, *On Revolution* (New York: Penguin, 1977), 177–78.

to the basic institutions, "values," and practices of American social, political, and economic existence[152]—that neutrality in the political sphere is not possible, and therefore that religion will simply take a diabolical form to the extent that the illusion is perpetuated.[153] But, even if it were possible to purify the political realm of religion, it would not in the least be desirable: it would require a radical reconception of the human being,

---

152 On the divinizing of the founding fathers and their founding deeds, see the fascinating book by Catherine Albanese, *Sons of the Fathers: The Civil Religion of the American Revolution* (Philadelphia: Temple University Press, 1977); for an argument regarding America now, see Peter Simpson, "Theocracy's Challenge," in *Challenging Theocracy: Ancient Lessons for Global Politics*, ed. David Edward Tabachnick, Toivo Koivukoski, and Herminio Meireles Teixeira (Toronto: University of Toronto Press, 2018), 195–216.

153 Exposing the non-neutrality of the liberal state was a regular theme in my father's work: see, for example, David L. Schindler, "Religious Freedom, Truth, and American Liberalism: Another Look at John Courtney Murray," *Communio* (Winter 1994): 696-741.

and the radical impoverishment of what is arguably *the* central reality of human existence, our being together in community, a being together that inevitably involves the effective presence of God.

There is scarcely a more deeply ingrained assumption in modern consciousness than the essential "secularity" of worldly affairs, whether one celebrates this fact or deplores it and then goes on to insist that religion must therefore deliberately be added by pious individuals.[154] If religion is added, this is taken to be something over and above the natural reality of politics, and thus something that either gratuitously supplements it or else distorts it. In light of the assumption that politics is "naturally" neutral, one tends to think that, if people in the past have tended to "sacralize" kingship as a matter of its nature, it is for psychological reasons or moral failings of some sort—namely, people tend to divinize those on whom they depend; rulers desire

---

154 See Andrew Willard Jones, *Before Church and State* (Steubenville, OH: Emmaus Academic Press, 2017), 1–32.

glory and power,[155] and so encourage or even actively enforce this; and both sides of the relation seek thereby to exercise some control over God. Because we are sinful, we cannot help but constantly fall to the temptation of idolatry, and if "the city is the soul writ large," then civil religion is idolatry writ large. But, if it is true that natural desires are more or less always distorted by sin, it remains the case that it is not just necessary, but altogether good in principle, to see the ruling power as able by virtue of his office to bring the presence of God to the city—not as an extraneous addition, but as enabling that presence to be properly recognized in an objective, institutionalized, and publicly

155 One of the more sophisticated and profound accounts of the "mixing" of politics and religious symbols of glory can be found in Giorgio Agamben, *The Kingdom and the Glory: For a Theological Genealogy of Economy and Government* (Stanford: Stanford University Press, 2011). Agamben approaches the matter from the perspective of what one might call a "hermeneutics of suspicion," but his observations are quite valuable.

established—that is, quasi-sacramental—
way. In other words, fallenness is expressed
not in the tendency to sacralize kingship, but
in the tendency *falsely* to *divinize* the king,
which is a wholly different phenomenon.[156]
Sacralizing kingship is inserting royal power
into the sacramental order safeguarded by
the Church, the order of the cosmos in the divine providence of history; divinizing the
king is an abstraction of royal power from
any encompassing order, and so unleashing
it from any real responsibility. Again, the
presence of God that is mediated by the ruling power is, to be sure, different from the actual sacramental presence directly brought by
the Church. At the same time, we would like
to suggest that the "natural" presence of God
in the city is necessary for the sacramental
presence brought by the Church to pervade

156 William McCormick, for example, identifies the
    tendency to recognize the sacred character of
    the ruler as "theocracy," and explains it as a
    constant temptation by virtue of our sinful con-
    dition: *The Christian Structure of Politics: The De
    Regno of Thomas Aquinas* (Washington, DC: CUA
    Press, 2021).

the whole of human existence as it is meant
to do, reaching into the very marrow of the
bones of a culture.

Political authority, properly understood,
is comprehensive, not in the sense of micro-
managing, i.e., intruding into each and every
human activity and directing it to the end the
authority itself dictates, as we tend to think
in our essentially totalitarian conception of
sovereignty.[157] Instead, it is comprehensive as
making explicit and effective the common
good that is inevitably aimed at implicitly
in all human action. Political authority
thus "comprehends" all human activities
and agents by opening up the relation to the

157 According to the classic definition of sovereignty formulated by Max Weber, "the state is
the form of human community that (successfully) lays claim to the monopoly on legitimate
physical violence." See Weber, *The Vocation Lectures* (Indianapolis, Hackett Publishing Com-
pany 2004), 33. If political rule is the exercise of
sovereignty, and sovereignty is interpreted as a
monopoly on coercive power, to accord a comprehensiveness to political rule would amount
to the establishment of a police state without
any limit to its jurisdiction over human life.

common good by which each person is an immediate sharer in that good as well as an indispensable member of the community. At the beginning of this chapter, we recalled the traditional neoplatonic view, articulated by Thomas Aquinas, that every agent loves the good of the whole *more than* it loves its own good, but loves that whole *in* its love for its own. Putting these two observations together, we can say that it is precisely political authority that allows this paradoxical intertwining of the private and the public, the proper and the common, to be properly realized and sustained. The reality of a truly political authority is an objective condition for the realization of man's natural desire. As Aquinas says in the *De Regno*, it is natural for individuals to pursue their proper good, which is why it is necessary that there be an office that has responsibility for the common good as such. But it is also the case that man has a natural desire for the common good that exceeds his individual good (even as a dimension within that individual good, as we argued above). Only if this common good is *effectively* present as such do we have an actual community, and so it is the filling of the office with an actual person, a concrete agent, that makes the community real, as something more than a collection of self-interested individuals.[158] This is how the political authority liberates, so to speak, the *common* dimension of the good implicit in individual human activity. Outside of real community, the paradox implicit in human desire and action, of loving the whole in loving oneself and vice versa, falls apart into a dialectical interplay of egoism and altruism.

But we can now add that the political authority not only brings out the common dimension of the good loved in each case, he thereby also brings out the *religious* dimension that is inseparably bound up with the commonality. God is always effectively present whenever activity concerns the common good in its transcendent reality as common. The presence of God, which characterizes all

---

158 Aristotle compares the reduction of common life to a coincidence of private goods to living like cattle feeding at a trough: *NE* IX.9.1170b12-14; cf., *Politics*, III.9.1280b30-32.

beings "innermostly," and especially human beings as *imagines dei*, becomes *properly religious* in the real community of a people. It is thus, by making effective the common good at the basis of common life, that the ruling power liberates and grants objective substance to the religious dimension, so to speak, in all human activity.

God is therefore present in the city in a manner analogous to his presence in sacramental marriage. The "ecclesial" character of the sacrament in marriage is not an extrinsic "overlay," which adds a religious meaning to an otherwise wholly natural or "secular" reality, but enters into, becomes expressive of, and thus genuinely *transforms*, the natural reality of marriage. The Church becomes effective *in* the marriage without eliminating its reality *as* marriage—indeed, rather than eliminate it, participation in the sacramental order of the Church affirms and liberates that reality. It can do so because the spouses are baptized, and so already actual participants in the sacramental order. But the Catholic Church has come to recognize that the sacramental character does not simply come from the sum of two baptized Christians; instead, the sacramental character is more than this sum, and so requires the *essentially public* witness of the official minister of the Church: the sacramental character arrives, thus, simultaneously from above and from below. This simultaneity is why the individual's relation to God is thus transformed into a communal celebration of that presence. The spouses of course retain an individual relation to God, interior to each as a person, but this interior relation is permanently made real—*realized*—in the sacramental union, wherein it is recapitulated in a new way that is both natural and ecclesial at once. The "locus" of their holiness, their Christian discipleship, has now changed, and changed forever: the spouses are enabled to share in a social holiness, that is, in holiness as institutional communion in the body of Christ.

We are proposing that there is something analogous in political community, properly understood, even though political community is not a sacramental union *per se*. Nevertheless, the city is the *real*-ization of a whole, a kind of supra-individual unity in which the members participate, and this unity gives rise to a new and now properly human relation to God. The city, too, presents its own kind of social form of holiness, an institutional communion in the good, and ultimately in God.[159] The presence of God arrives in the city, so to speak, simultaneously from above and from below: God is present naturally in each individual as a human person, and only thereby can he be properly "introduced" in and through the ruling power; and this introduction takes the form, so to speak, of mirroring back to individuals the reality of their interior relation to God, thus making it truly *real* for the first time—that is, making it a *res*, a *res publica*, which is an actual, objective, official "thing" in the world that all may see, acknowledge, and celebrate. If the relation to God is good, this shared relation is *very good*; it is a part of

159 Speaking of the city in medieval Italy, Thompson writes "Communal holiness flourished in community; it was social," *Cities of God*, 194.

the *eu zēn*, the elevated well-being, that Aristotle said belongs to the city.[160] And, of course, when we are speaking of the relation to God, the "very good," for all of its gratuitous elevation, is the proper human norm.

In the contemporary world, those that want to recall the essential place of God in our lives typically champion the "right to religious freedom." But to the extent that this is conceived merely as a protection for private belief or worship-preference, it represents a betrayal of our nature as *homo religiosus*. A genuine response to the political nihilism that has quite evidently overtaken our common existence, requires an expansion of our political, philosophical, and theological imagination, so that we might recognize, once again, that if we do indeed encounter God in the innermost, secret depth of our hearts, it is only because we encounter him also in the life of the city.

160 Aristotle, *Politics*, III.9.1280a30-33.

Chapter Three
The Glory of God Is the City Fully Alive: On the Soul and Body of Politics

In the *De Regno*, Aquinas indicates the king's literally extraordinary role of communicating the presence of God in the very act of constituting the city by presenting the king as standing in "loco dei."[161] He elaborates the content of the king's special office thus: "he is to be in the kingdom what the soul is in the body and what God is in the world" (*sit in regno sicut in corpore anima et sicut Deus in mundo*).[162] The metaphor of the

---

161 Aquinas, *De Regno*, I.13 [95].
162 Ibid.

soul's relation to the body is no doubt the most prominent metaphor employed in pre-modern political thought to characterize the nature of ruling power. Typically, the metaphor is interpreted simply *as* a metaphor, and indeed limited to a description of the order of operation, which is to say limited to spelling out the hierarchy of different powers in their exercise. But our reflections thus far suggest that the claim can be understood as carrying a certain ontological weight. What we intend to do in this final chapter is to interpret this metaphor as a genuine analogy and to give it most fundamentally an ontological sense, which is appropriate for our effort at a political metaphysics. We will see that the particular details of Aquinas's interpretation of the body-soul relationship cast a light on the nature of political authority that reveals dimensions that might otherwise lie hidden.

If Aquinas is able to allude to the body-soul relation to make such a fundamental point about God's presence and the king's role without laying out any extensive argument in the *De regno*, it is no doubt because the analogy is no innovation of his own, but represents a long tradition. The traditional use of the body-soul analogy in relation to politics is multidimensional. On the one hand, it expresses the distinctive way that a ruler can be present throughout his kingdom without having to be physically in every place at the same time[163]—just as the soul is present throughout the body as a whole in each and every part.[164] In this respect, the kingdom represents something like the king's "second body," a mystical one standing over against the king's physical body,[165] but intelligible by analogy to the Church in relation to Christ.[166] On the other

163 Aquinas, *ST* 1.8.3.
164 Aquinas, *ST*, 1.76.8; cf., *De anima*, 10.
165 Ernst Kantorowicz presents the history of the notion in his classic work *The King's Two Bodies: A Study in Medieval Political Theology* (Princeton: Princeton University Press, 2016).
166 See Henri de Lubac, *Corpus Mysticum* (Notre Dame, IN: University of Notre Dame Press, 2007). Kantorowicz was inspired by de Lubac in his interpretation of medieval political theology.

hand, the body-soul analogy is used to describe the relation between the temporal order of the earthly city and the spiritual order of the Church. This is a principal theme, for example, of John of Salisbury's twelfth-century *Polycraticus*, which is generally recognized as the first work of political philosophy in the Middle Ages.[167] But the analogy is virtually as old as Christianity itself, appearing in the *Letter to Diognetus* (circa AD 130), for example, to characterize the way Christians are present in the world.[168] More broadly speaking, the body-soul relation has been used to illuminate God's relation to the cosmos, as we see in the fundamental theme of the "World Soul" in neoplatonic and stoic philosophy, originating, more or less, with Plato's *Timaeus*, but revived in a direct way in the Renaissance and borne into the modern era with Spinoza and

---

167 John of Salisbury, *Policraticus*, ed. Cary J. Nederman (Cambridge: Cambridge University Press, 1990), Editor's Introduction, xv.

168 Clayton N. Jefford, *The Epistle to Diognetus*, ed. By N. Brox et al. (Oxford: Oxford University Press, 2013).

German Idealism.[169] The cosmos as a whole is God's body, animated by the Spirit of God. Finally, it bears remarking that this analogy, like all analogies, goes both ways, so to speak, which means that the complex unity of the political order, for example, can illuminate the nature of the relation between body and soul in the individual human being: the order of the "parts" of the individual human being can be likened to the order of the classes of people in a city. This, of course, is also a classic theme in Western thought.[170]

169 See Hans Urs von Balthasar, *Theologic*, vol. 3: *The Spirit of Truth* (San Francisco: Ignatius Press, 2000), 421. Recovering the theme of the "world soul" was a central aim of Schelling's *Natur-philosophie*: see his *Bruno: On the Natural and the Divine Principle of Things* (Albany, NY: SUNY Press, 1984). For a contemporary revival of this effort, see David Fideler, *Restoring the Soul of the World* (Rochester, VT: Inner Traditions, 2007).

170 In Plato, the theme is articulated according to "parts of the soul," rather than "parts of the body," but the soul is obviously differentiated in this way by its relationship to the body: this is the basic focus of the first part (after the prologue of book I) of his *Republic*: bks II-IV. St.

It is impossible to pursue all of these dimensions in depth, though doing so would no doubt be enormously helpful. We nevertheless mention all of them here in order to identify the proper context for our particular line of inquiry, and also to bring out the depth of implications of the theme we are pursuing. We will focus specifically in the following on the relation between the ruler and the city, and even more basically on the relation between what is called the spiritual and the temporal orders, because our principal theme is the presence of God in the city; but we wish to state two assumptions that form the background of our present reflection, both guiding and inspiring it. First, to say that the four relations mentioned—God and world, Church and city, king and kingdom, and soul and body in the individual man—are related analogically is to say both

Paul uses the analogy to talk about the Church: 1 Cor 12:12-27; cf., Romans 12:5. The theme finds a nice expression in Shakespeare's presentation of the Roman sense of political order: see *Coriolanus* I.1.96-163.

that there is something like a common pattern or structure running through all of these pairs of terms, and also that the common pattern is not univocal, but turns up in a radically different way in each case.[171] Moreover, the difference in each case is not a threat to the unity between and among them, but in fact informs each, so that we could say one would have to understand all of these relations in their uniqueness in order to understand each one properly in particular. In other words, it is not just that reflection on

---

171 It bears remarking that the radical difference is a matter of principle, but also that the difference will be further differentiated, so to speak, in the historical realization of the principle; the historical realization introduces the aspect of disorder we mentioned in chapter one. Disorder cannot be properly managed simply through the re-imposition of order, but requires the concrete deliberation of prudence (properly interpreted: see my chapter, "Prudence and Tragedy," *Politics of the Real*, 293–311). Acknowledging this difference, as explained above in chapter one, we are nonetheless focusing our attention here on the principle rather than on the historical realization.

the body-soul relation helps us to understand the relation between God and the world, for example, but also that we ultimately need to understand the God-world relation in order properly to grasp the relation between body and soul.

The second assumption is closely related to this first. To refer to these complex sets of relations as analogous is to make a fully ontological, and not just an epistemological or semiotic, claim; in other words, we are affirming not just that the various pairs of terms happen to have certain features in common, in spite of complete ontological independence from each other, so that it may possibly be helpful (or not) to compare them using a "metaphor." Instead, our claim is that these pairs are ontologically bound to each other, so to speak; they are interrelated in something like an "organic" fashion, which implies that the way we understand, and relate to, any one of them, will bear on our relation to all the others, and a disorder in one will tend to disorder the rest. More hopefully, the healing of one will tend to restore the rest. For example, a disordered interpretation of the relation between the body and the soul will imply a problematic sense of community and political order, a fragmentary sense of the Church in relation to human culture, and most profoundly a disobedience, whether wittingly or not, to God.[172] While this may seem a massive assumption to make, especially without an elaborate defense in the present context,[173] we submit that something of this interconnectedness, articulated explicitly by Plato but already as an old tradition,[174] has been

---

172 The theme of man and the enactment of the body-soul relation as an interpretation of being, and implicitly of God, is the basic theme of part II of Ulrich's *Homo Abyssus*. For the directly political dimension of this theme, see "Politische Macht," 398.

173 A much more in-depth elaboration of this point can be found in *Freedom from Reality* and *Politics of the Real*.

174 Plato expresses an essential aspect of this in the *Gorgias*, where, referring to a belief that has always been held by "wise men," he presents the cosmos as constituting a world-order precisely in the form of a friendship or communion, in which both man and the gods share. Participat-

taken for granted by apparently all pre-modern cultures from the East to the West.[175] In that respect, the burden of proof arguably lies more heavily on the contemporary thinking that would deny this connection.

However that may be, if these guiding assumptions are true, and the connection among these things is not a mere metaphor, which joins accidentally similar features by virtue of a fiction, it implies that a deeper interpretation of the reality of one pair will shed light on the rest. Taking this for granted here, we intend in the present chapter to explore in some detail the metaphysical interpretation of

ing in this friendship, he explains, requires a cultivation of the virtues in oneself and in the political sphere, as Socrates insists in another part of the dialogue: see *Gorgias*, 507e-508a, 504b, 521d. We noted earlier the ontological sense given to the theme of justice beginning already with Anaximander.

175 A memorable, if not very philosophically sophisticated, presentation of this premodern view can be found in Arthur Oncken Lovejoy, *The Great Chain of Being* (Cambridge, Mass.: Harvard University Press, 1976), based on the William James lectures delivered in 1933.

the body-soul relation offered by Thomas Aquinas, an interpretation that no doubt represents the culmination of the classic tradition on this theme. Aquinas's anthropology may be succinctly characterized as uniting the apparently divergent views of Plato and Aristotle, within a vision of God's creation *ex nihilo*. He thus reconciles a radical independence of the soul with an affirmation of the genuine unity of the human animal, and so an appreciation of the fully temporal and physical dimension of human existence. This synthesis will prove fruitful in the political sphere.

On the one hand, Aquinas insists, with Plato, on the radical transcendence of the spiritual soul in relation to the body, a transcendence that is so much a part of the *essence* of the soul that the soul is capable of existing by itself, in separation from the body.[176] Now, in contrast to the Franciscan theologians of the time—such as Bonaventure, who thought that such a separate existence required the soul to be a hylomorphic

176 Aquinas, *ST* 1.75.2ad6.

substance unto itself, which is to say a "form-matter" unity by itself, and in independence from the body[177]—Aquinas sought a way to affirm the genuine transcendence, and so relative independence, of the soul without compromising the *real unity* between soul and body, which was not so evident in Bonaventure's thought on this matter. A relation between one complete hylomorphic substance (the soul) and another (the body) can only ever be an accidental coincidence of two essentially separate *things*, no matter how necessary one might wish to make the accident.[178] (One can imagine, without much difficulty, the implications of

---

177 See Etienne Gilson, *The Philosophy of Bonaventure* (New York: Sheed and Ward, 1938), 315–40.

178 We do not mean here to pronounce a definitive judgment on Bonaventure's conception of the unity of man. For an argument showing how Bonaventure can account for body and soul being one substance (even as distinct substances in themselves) by virtue of the soul's "unibility," see Thomas Osborne, Jr., "Unibilitas: The Key to Bonaventure's Understanding of Human Nature," *Journal of the History of Philosophy* 37.2 (April 1999): 227–50.

an anthropology along these lines for the conception of the Church-state relation.) A coincidence of two relatively complete entities can never form a single substance, which is what Aquinas took *man* to be, since man is a creature that did not fall into corporeality, as the various versions of Gnosticism (and Origenism) have it, but was created, and so intended by God, from the beginning and all the way to the end, as an *essentially* embodied spirit.[179] Aquinas therefore took over the Aristotelian notion that the soul is the form of the body, which means that the soul and body together form one *thing*, an "unum per se," just as wax and the shape it possesses are one thing.[180]

---

179 Aquinas, ST, 1.90.4: "For it is clear that God made the first things in their perfect natural state, as their species required. Now the soul, as a part of human nature, has its natural perfection only as united to the body. Therefore it would have been unfitting for the soul to be created without the body."

180 A substance is a "unum per se et non secundum accidens," *Commentary on Metaphysics*, IV, lectio 2 [554]; *Commentary on the Soul*, II, lectio 1 [234].

At first it seems that these two affirmations—that the soul can exist in itself as a separate substance or thing and that the body and soul together are not a coincidence of two separate things but a single reality, a single substance—exclude each other essentially, such that to affirm them both is to contradict oneself. But considering how Aquinas is able to avoid this contradiction will turn out to cast a brilliant light into the political problem. Aquinas can avoid the contradiction in his anthropology because of a principle derived from his metaphysics, to which neither Plato nor Aristotle had (direct) access, namely, the principle of *esse*, the act of being, really distinct from both form and matter, without being some "thing" existing apart from them.[181] For Aquinas, in harmony with Plato but at least apparently in contrast to Aristotle, it *is* possible to have a pure form, a form without matter, that exists in reality, and not only in the

---

181 For a nuanced discussion of created *esse* as a distinct principle, most perfect, but realized only in created things, see David L. Schindler, *The Generosity of Creation* (Washington, D.C.: Humanum Academic Press, 2018).

intellect: we find such forms, for example, in the angels, which according to Aquinas are "separate substances," that is, pure spirits without any "admixture" of matter.[182] But the reason such pure forms can be distinguished from God, a distinction that continually troubles Platonism,[183] is that pure forms are, for Aquinas, *not* pure actualities *simpliciter*, as God is, but are blends of potency and act, like all creatures, since they have a "composite" sort of being. Their composition, however, is not that of form and matter, as the standard Aristotelianism would have it, and as the early Franciscans appear to have assumed was the only way to conceive composition; instead, it is a composition of a higher order, namely, a composition of essence and existence.[184] In this

---

182 Aquinas, *De spiritualibus creaturis*, 1.

183 Ferdinand Ulrich presents a profound reflection on the eternity of forms problem, which recurs in Christianity as the problem of the relative independence of the divine ideas from the divine intellect: see, for example, *Homo Abyssus*, 135–46.

184 Aquinas, ST 1.75.5ad4: "in intellectual substances there is a composition of actuality and potentiality, not indeed of matter and form, but

case pure form is not, without qualification, itself the reason for its own existence, but the immaterial essence still represents potency in relation to *esse*, the act of being by which the form exists.[185]

Let us appreciate the subtlety of this point. Aquinas does affirm that a pure form, such as an angel, and more directly relevant for us, the human soul, does indeed exist by virtue of itself, "per se," which is to say it exists by nature.[186] It is impossible for there to be a pure form that does not exist *necessarily* in this sense, which is to say, *if* such a form

---

of form and participated existence"; cf., 1.50.2ad3.

185 See for example ST 1.90.2ad1: "The soul's simple essence is as the material element, while its participated existence [esse] is its formal element."

186 ST 1.75.6: "It is clear that what belongs to a thing by virtue of itself is inseparable from it; but existence belongs to a [self-subsisting form, such as the human soul], which is an act, by virtue of itself. . . . But it is impossible for a form to be separated from itself; and therefore it is impossible for a subsistent form to cease to exist."

exists, it exists *necessarily*: "participated existence necessarily co-exists with the soul's essence, because existence naturally follows the form."[187] But, for Aquinas, to say this does not mean that such a form simply *is* its being. This can be said only of God.[188] Instead, an essentially spiritual creature exists *per se*, but it does so by virtue of a principle distinct from itself, such that we can affirm a "real distinction" between essence and *esse* even within perfect unity, a unity that is indeed so perfect we can legitimately say the soul exists by virtue of its own essence, which is what existence "per se" effectively means.[189] Why is such a subtle distinction so important? It is important because it is *just this* difference of the soul from its being that allows Aquinas to affirm a profound ontological unity between

187 ST 1.90.2ad1.

188 See *De pot.*, 7.2.corpus and ad 5.

189 "Effectively" because there remains a paradox here, which is the very point we are seeking to make: the soul exists necessarily by virtue of its existing essence (not its essence simply speaking, which may be considered for example as an *a priori* logical possibility).

soul and body in the human animal without compromising the soul's essential transcendence of the body, and the "natural immortality" this transcendence implies. When Aquinas asks how the soul and body are able to form together a single being, an "unum per se," he gives this pregnant response: "the soul communicates that existence in which it subsists to the corporeal matter, out of which and the intellectual soul there results unity of existence: so that the existence of the whole composite is also the existence of the soul."[190] That form gives being to matter is not strange; this is in fact a standard principle in scholastic thought, which Aquinas accepts: *forma dat esse*.[191] What is unique here—and

---

190 Aquinas, ST 1.76.1ad5. Cf., *De anima*, 1ad17: "While the act of existing is the most formal of all principles, it is also the most communicable, although it is not shared in the same measure both by inferior beings and by superior ones. Hence the body shares in the soul's act of existing, but not as perfectly as the soul does."

191 As Aquinas puts it, "the form is the principle of existence": ST 1.76.2. See Sylvain Roudaut, "Forma Dat Esse: Tracking the Rise and Fall of

the point is of *decisive* importance, worth reflecting on at great length—is that the *esse*
that the "*forma dat*," in this case, is in a certain
respect the same as the form, at least in the
sense that it belongs to the form by virtue of
its essence or inner logic; as we recall, the soul
exists *per se*, and not merely *per accidens*.
When the soul gives being to the body, we
ought to understand this, on the one hand, as
giving to the body, not something simply extrinsic to the soul, but the soul's very self, its
own inner being, which is why the two fundamentally can be one, united so to speak in
a genuinely intimate way, and, on the other
hand, as giving the body more than itself, insofar as the *esse* it gives remains "really distinct" from it, which is why the union does
not absorb the body into the soul (or vice
versa), but liberates it so to speak in its integrity as radically different from soul.[192] In

Formal Causality," *History of Philosophy & Logical Analysis* 23 (2020): 423–46, an article that
presents the evolution of this universally affirmed axiom in medieval thought.

192 We see here, incidentally, one of the reasons we
need to understand God's creation of the world

giving being, the soul is both giving itself and giving the body *to be*, i.e., to be a body. Only in human beings do we have such a remarkable coincidence of such apparently opposing principles: angels are their being in a certain respect, but do not give that being to a body, and all sub-human creatures *are* not their being in this intrinsic way, since they do not possess a spiritual, i.e., self-subsistent, form as soul.[193]

Before we turn to see what light this sheds on the relation between God and the city, we need to unfold two dimensions of this remarkable and paradoxical relationship. First, we must ask what it means exactly for the soul to give being to the body, and, second, we must ask how God "fits in," so to speak, to this gift. Regarding the first point, we must first note that this giving of being is different from a *creatio ex nihilo*, in

in order properly to understand the soul's analogous gift of being to the body: only creation suffices to bring to light the soul's gift of being *to* the body, as the body's very own, which it nevertheless possesses in union with the soul.

193 Aquinas, ST 1.75.7.

which God gives being to the whole cosmos and everything in it *tout court*.[194] The soul does not *create* the body; instead, it presupposes the existence of the material components, which, not living in themselves, receive life by virtue of the relation to the soul.[195] On the other hand, however, this

194 Aquinas describes creation as the "emanatio totius entis a causa universali, quae est Deus": ST 1.45.1.

195 See William McCormick, S.J., *The Christian Structure of Politics* (Washington, DC: CUA Press, 2022), 158. McCormick emphasizes this point in his discussion of the king as analogous to God and the soul. But he does not do justice to the full analogy in the sense we are attempting to explicate it here: the soul certainly does not create the body, but it also does not simply come upon the body as already there, so to speak. Instead, it gives rise to the bodiliness of the body, as it were, by offering it the form that allows it to be a body in the first place, and not simply a heap of materials. The soul's relation to the body is therefore analogous to God's relation to the world he creates; we are going to argue that the ruler's relation to the city (and the Church's relation to the political order) is similarly analogous.

does not mean that, prior to the "infusion" of the soul, the body is just *there*, qua body, with everything it needs to live, simply awaiting the "spark" to set it all in motion (as we may be inclined to think, for example, from a Franciscan perspective that posits the body as having a form distinct from the soul). Instead, a body *is* by definition a living thing; it is not a (dead) encasement of a living thing. To deprive a body of life is to make it something *other* than a body—specifically, a "heap," a merely coincidental collection of parts, which may still stick together for a short expanse of time, but will very soon, in fact immediately, begin to fall apart, once the soul is absent. It does so because there is no longer anything to hold it together such that it can actually *be* a body. A "dead body" is an oxymoron, and if criminal detectives speak of the corpse in these terms as they work on a case, they do so only metaphorically.[196]

---

196 Aristotle explains that, for example, the hand of a dead body is a hand only in an equivocal sense (like a stone hand): *Politics*, I.2.1253a20-25; cf., *De anima*, II.1. Aquinas makes the same point in ST 1.76.8.

According to Aquinas, following Aristotle here, we must not only define the body as that which "has life potentially within it,"[197] we must also say that this potency for life does not precede the body's relation to soul, as a fully wired house that just needs the switch flipped to become illuminated. Instead, the potency is itself derived from the soul.[198] Note the subtlety again: the soul not only gives life to the body, it gives to the body, so to speak,[199] the capacity to receive that life, and if such a capacity defines the body, it is finally the soul that makes the material elements into a body. This emphatically *does not* mean, however, that the body is a mere function or extension of the soul. Instead, the body, as matter, and indeed as

197 Aquinas, ST 1.76.4ad1.
198 It is "by the soul," Aquinas says, that the body "is a body, and is organic, and has life potentially": ST 1.76.4ad1.
199 It does not give this to the body as one thing giving to another thing a third reality; instead, the potency that defines the body is possessed by virtue of the soul, so that the soul is the principle of that potency, even if it is not the *subject* of the potency.

matter received in some sense from the outside world, is radically different from the
soul, and remains such even in the living
man. The subsistent *unity* of soul and body
in man never means a confusion of the two,
for Aquinas, because this unity coincides
with a radical difference between them.

The crucial point is that the body *has*
this difference from the soul only *inside* the
relation to the soul; the body can be distinct
from the soul qua body, rather than qua an
assortment of material elements, only if it is
united to the soul, and its potency to receive
life only exists inside of its participation in
the life it actually receives.[200] But because

200 ST 1.76.6: "Now the first among all acts is exis-
      tence. Therefore, it is impossible for matter to
      be apprehended as hot, or as having quantity,
      before it is actual. But matter has actual exis-
      tence by the substantial form, which makes it to
      exist absolutely, as we have said above. Where-
      fore it is impossible for any accidental disposi-
      tions to pre-exist in matter before the
      substantial form, and consequently before the
      soul." Cf., 1.76.8: "on the withdrawal of the
      soul, no part of the body retains its proper ac-
      tion."

this absolute priority of the soul does *not* make the body simply a part of itself, this means that, although the soul gives life to the body, it is not the soul that pumps the blood,[201] that digests the food, that processes the sensible and irascible stimulations that constitute all of the activities of life. Instead, the body does *all* of these, in some respect, "of itself," but this self-actuation is itself a capacity received from the soul. In short, the body governs itself because it is governed by the soul. It participates in the "ruling function" of the soul in a specifically bodily way, which is to say that the body is properly speaking an *analogous* expression of the soul. This is why Aquinas's affirmation that the soul contains the body, rather than the reverse (which is

---

201 This point must be qualified, for there is a sense in which the soul *does* pump the blood, insofar as it is the soul, according to Aquinas, that moves the heart, and through the heart moves the rest of the body, though of course it does so, not in a mechanistic way, but in a properly organic way: the soul remains also present throughout the body: see *De anima*, 9ad13.

how all dualistic thinking imagines things),[202] does not imply that the soul exercises a kind of despotic control over everything, "micro-managing" the activities of life in all of their extraordinarily differentiated detail. We can speak of the life *of the body* in a very real sense, intending this point in all of the depths of the subjective genitive, and still say that it is in fact *the soul* that is the life of the body.

But we can also say, as for example John of Salisbury does in his own exposition of the analogy, that God is the life of the soul.[203] This leads us to the second point. Precisely because the human soul is rational or spiritual, which is to say it is a pure form that does indeed participate in existence as something different from itself, but does so *per se*, it cannot come into being as a result of any change that occurs inside of creation, or in other

---

202 "It cannot be said that [body and soul] are united by the one body; because rather does the soul contain the body and make it one than the reverse": ST 1.76.3.

203 See John of Salisbury, *Policraticus* III.1 (Nederman, 14–16).

words any event in the world, but must be created immediately by God.[204] The human soul's immediate relation to God, as we described already in chapter two, is constitutive of both the being and the operation of the soul, which is to say that God remains profoundly present in all that the soul is and does. When Aquinas affirms the traditional teaching of the soul's being made "in the image of God," he explains this—and so confirms our interpretation of analogy above—not principally by indicating certain common features (i.e., the distinct powers of the one soul are like the Persons of the Trinity), but even more fundamentally by bringing this essential presence to light: just as God knows and loves Himself, the human soul knows and loves . . . *God*.[205] The (causal) ontological

---

204 ST 1.90.2. Cf., *De anima* 1ad2: "the soul receives its act of existence from God as from an active principle."

205 ST 1.93.4. Note, this does not exclude the analogical character of the soul's knowing and loving itself; it simply roots this formal likeness character in the deeper ontological, causal presence of God.

connection founds the formal similarity. It follows from this ontological connection that the soul's communication of its existence to the body is at the same time a communication of the distinctive presence of God. Here, again, we are going beyond the explicit statements of Aquinas but it is only in order to remain faithful to their logic. Let us recall that all power comes from God: this would include the body's power to receive life. John of Salisbury makes the same point, quoting a contemporary poet who is in turn quoting St. Augustine: "God is the life of the soul, and the soul the life of the body; the one dissolves when the other flees, lost when it is undermined by God."[206] If the soul's communication of God to the body happens already implicitly in the very existence of the living human being, it occurs more explicitly and directly in the fulfillment of that existence in the direct vision of God in the eschaton: "in

---

206 *Policraticus*, 14. According to Augustine, "Just as the whole life of the body is the soul, so the blessed life of the soul is God," *De lib. arb.*, 2.16.41; cf., *City of God*, 13.24.6.

the final state, after the resurrection, the soul will, to a certain extent, communicate to the body what properly belongs to itself as spirit; immortality to everyone, impassibility, glory, and power to the good, whose bodies will be called *spiritual*."[207] The *spiritual* life, or in other words being in the mode of openness to goodness, truth, and beauty in their unrestricted senses, which turns out ultimately to belong not just to the soul but *also* to the body, would represent a violence to essentially opaque, dumb "stuff," if the presence of God were not, so to speak, congenital to the body, from the beginning.[208]

Having unfolded, however briefly, basic

---

207 ST 1.97.3. St. Paul speaks of course of "glorifying God in our bodies": Phil 1:20. Note that "glory," in Aquinas, means participation in the inner life of God. On the distinction between the state of nature, grace, and glory, see Benjamin Smith, "Imago Dei: Nature, Grace, and Glory according to Aquinas," in *A Companion to Medieval Christian Humanism*, ed. John P. Bequette (Leiden: Brill, 2016), 212–31.

208 Aquinas argues that, in fact, the very first human body had to be created immediately by God, just like the soul: ST 1.92.2.

dimensions of Aquinas's interpretation of the body-soul relation, we may now turn to consider what light it sheds on political order. We noted the classic analogy, according to which the relation between the temporal order of the city and the spiritual order governed by the Church is related as body to soul. Typically, this is interpreted as a metaphor indicating hierarchical orders of authority or ruling power, as well as setting off realms of jurisdiction, so to speak.[209] But we have seen that, prior to the question of governance, the relation between soul and body concerns *being* and *life*; in other words, it concerns the first act of the human substance and only thus also the second act. The soul communicates the being that belongs to it by its very nature, but which it also receives immediately from God, to the body, so that the body can be truly itself, a living body, capable of all the operations essential to it as a living body. Note what is being excluded in this claim: it

209 This is how Aquinas appears to present the matter, for example, in his early work: *II Sent.* D.44, q.3, a.4.

is not the case that the body already exists in itself prior to the relation to the soul, even in the barest material sense. While it is true that the soul does not create, of itself, the matter of the body, but presupposes the existence of the material components, these components exist *as a physical body* only insofar as they are gathered together, so to speak, around the unity given by the soul. Similarly, the city does not first exist as a purely earthly reality, to which the "spiritual" dimension may (or may not) be added by the Church. This would assume a Cartesian, rather than a Thomistic, conception of the body-soul relation.[210] Instead, it can exist as a city, as a reality in the world, only insofar as it is gathered around the unity of a comprehensive common good, a common good, we have argued, that is as much spiritual as it is temporal, or in fact is more fundamentally

---

210 Note that this is precisely the point that De Lubac makes in his argument regarding the intrinsic unity, within difference, of nature and grace: "The Mystery of the Supernatural," in *Theology in History* (San Francisco: Ignatius Press, 1996), 288.

spiritual insofar as the only common good that suffices to generate a human city is one that is the same as the end of man, and what *distinguishes* man as man is his spiritual nature. Thus, the temporal operations of the city are not separate from the spiritual operations, but are themselves *essentially spiritual*, even in their temporality, and even apart from any distinctly eschatological considerations. To return to the terms of anthropology, the totally bodily function of digesting food, for instance, is a function that occurs only because the body is alive, which is to say only by virtue of the soul, because digestion is not just a purely physical movement of matter from one place to another, but the taking up of matter into the higher-level form of the human being.[211] Digestion is, in this sense, a

---

211 Consider the philosophical description of metabolism offered by Hans Jonas, *The Phenomenon of Life* (Evanston, IL: Northwestern University Press, 2000), 75–76. Aquinas presents matter as seeking form in this way: "the ultimate end of the whole process of generation is the human soul, and matter tends toward it as toward an ultimate form": SCG 3.22.7.

spiritual activity, even while being physical. By analogy, it is only because the city is, so to speak, fundamentally spiritual that it can properly regulate an economy, which is after all not just the purely rational, quantitative calculation of competing self-interests, but the interaction of *human beings* and the resources of the real world. A city that brackets out the *truth* of man, which is to say a city that establishes ignorance about the nature and destiny of the human person as a matter of policy, cannot possibly regulate the economy correctly. Economics is as much a spiritual reality as it is a temporal reality—or indeed quite obviously is *even more* spiritual than temporal.[212]

212 This point, which John Ruskin insisted on so vehemently at the birth of the "dismal science" of economics in the nineteenth century (see his *Unto this Last* [New York: Penguin, 1986]), has increasingly been returning to the attention in some form at any rate of mainstream economists. On this score, see the argument presented by Mary Hirschfeld, *Aquinas and the Market: Toward a Humane Economy* (Cambridge, Mass.: Harvard University Press, 2018).

Let us spell this out further. It is not the case that the soul enacts a single, strictly "spiritual" function, alongside and juxtaposed to the various other functions of the body, which, as such, are *not* spiritual. The soul is not one of the parts of the body; it is not, as we explained above, "contained" inside the body as a discrete element of the whole. Instead, the *whole soul* is present in each of the parts and in all of them together, and thus pervades the body, to such an extent that we can say it is the soul that contains the body. It is only because of the presence of the whole soul in each part that the body can be a body, a complex system of living tissues and functions that are *internally* connected to each other: the parts can be so internally connected only because of the transcendent unity of the soul that mediates the parts to each other. By analogy, the Church, which represents the spiritual order, cannot be just one of the parts of the city; it cannot represent a single, discrete, strictly "spiritual" function juxtaposed to the temporal functions of the city. Instead, if there is, both in the human being and in the city, a strictly spiritual function (which of course there *is*), it is nevertheless the case that the Church pervades the whole of the city, giving genuinely human life to the city and enabling the various "temporal" functions of the city to be themselves life-giving. The Church can be said thus to contain the city in a manner analogous to the way in which the soul contains the body. To think that the city is something like a neutral, purely temporal organization, which makes space within itself—and thus necessarily on its own terms—for the religious life of its members, however they choose to live that life, whether that life be thought of as purely private belief or publicly enacted worship, is strictly speaking *non-sense*. Such a conception simply fails to understand what a city is, what the Church is, and what role religion plays in human life.

To say that the Church contains the city and pervades all of its activity, present as a whole in each of its parts, may sound like theocracy in its most extreme, not to say "extremist," sense. But this impression arises likewise as a result of the failure to grasp the body-soul relation and its analogous expression at this higher level. The soul does not intrude on the body or impose itself as one thing on another in the body's proper operations as one *thing* acting on another *thing*.[213] The soul does not "dictate" to the body the body's own functions, or, still worse, substitute itself for the body. As we already explained, the soul does not digest food; instead, the *body* does, even if it does only by virtue of its relation to the soul, and the body performs this act so much of itself that digestion can be described, at one level, wholly in material terms.[214] The

---

213 The soul, as spirit, i.e., as intellect and will, does indeed operate directly (*operatione per se*) in carrying out properly human acts, in which the body is involved in a much more purely instrumental way: ST 1.75.2. It would be very interesting to reflect on the significance of the distinctly co-operating functions of body and soul—sense experience and imagination in the cognitive order and passions and love in the appetitive order—in light of the political analogy.
214 We might compare this to E. F. Schumacher's observation that one can relate to the very same text, on the one hand, as markings on a page,

intrinsic relation to the soul does not make the function any less bodily, but in fact allows it properly to *be* bodily (rather than a mere chemical process, which could occur in a petri dish as well as anywhere else). By analogy, it is the truth of the human being, which as we have seen inescapably involves relation to God and is thus essentially religious, especially in its communal existence, a truth presented most directly by the Church (or more specifically: by the intellectual, cultural, and material inheritance safeguarded by the Church as much as by the Church as the sacramental presence of God), that allows the city to govern itself properly, in a genuinely human way. The Church does not rule over the city *per se*, but the city can rule itself (in the person of the governing power) only in the light of the spiritual dimensions introduced, as it were, by the Church. The Church can remain, in this respect, an institutional authority with

and, on the other, as a collection of words with meaning: see *A Guide for the Perplexed* (New York: HarperCollins, 2015).

respect to the city without directly ruling the city.[215] Here we see the significance of the fact that the body does not simply participate directly in the soul in the sense of being a mere extension of the soul (which will eventually be retracted, wholly reduced back to the soul), but receives *being* from the soul, a being that in one respect belongs to the soul by nature, but in another respect transcends the soul, as "really" distinct from the soul's essence, so as to be able to be given to what is *other* than the soul, namely, the body, in a way that definitively grounds its otherness inside of the real unity. The body has a reality of its own, but it has this reality only by virtue of the soul. The city has a reality of its own, a distinctive order of operation in which its authority is supreme, but it has this perfectly complete integrity only by virtue of the encompassing

215 This is arguably the point that is most fundamentally missed by contemporary integralists, who do not have a sufficiently analogical sense of ruling authority and so regularly reduce the terms of the question to the relative distribution of coercive power.

reality of the Church. The perfect unity between city and Church is what allows a perfect difference between them. We will return to this point, and deepen it, in just a moment.

One might object, at this point, that the strong claim being made for the necessary presence of the Church for the existence of the city, *as* city, insofar as it is a city, would seem to be belied by history, and indeed quite obviously so: there have been many cities, a countless number, that existed before the advent of Christianity, and there are still a countless number that exist today outside of any relation to the Church. In response, we can say first of all that there has not been, and there *cannot* be, any city that exists independently of a relation to God, and this is not just because God is present by nature everywhere. It is also because, as we have been arguing, there is a special relation between God and the city that is essential to any city qua city. A city is by its very nature a spiritual or religious reality.[216] Just as the body is

216 This is one of the essential themes of the classic,

always-already related to God even in its physical reality, which is why it can be elevated into a direct participation in the Trinitarian life of God, and indeed perfected rather than destroyed by that participation, so too is it the essentially religious reality of the city that opens it naturally to the Church, which is why the Church can pervade the city without compromising the city's wholly *earthly* reality. (It is also why the city can be elevated to become itself the realization of God's presence in creation, the New Jerusalem, the City of God.) We cannot pursue the question here, but it is not difficult to see that there will be a radical difference between cities that existed prior to Christian revelation, cities that exist in some sense as of yet outside the actual reach of the Church, and cities that have sought to *become* "secular," to purify themselves of their Christian inheritance for what are taken to be prudential political reasons of some sort, but which have a

path-breaking study by Numa Denis Fustel de Coulanges, *The Ancient City* (Garden City, NY: Doubleday-Anchor, n.d.).

natural tendency to become ideological programs. The former two can be truly, and naturally, religious, but the last will inevitably pervert and distort the religious dimension that will nevertheless essentially abide and be officially enforced. In this respect, at the very center of politics and the effort to understand the nature of a city is the need to come to terms with the history of the Church in the world.[217]

However that may be, it is essential that we appreciate the full dimensions of the difference between the Church and the city even in their essential unity, and reflecting further on the body-soul relation helps us do just that. We suggested that in communicating *being* to the body, the soul also communicates God. Just as the body, through the soul's communication, receives its own being, so that we may say that the body exists as a reality in itself, which at the same time is a being it shares with

---

217 This is the premise of the new book by Andrew Willard Jones, *The Two Cities: A History of Christian Politics* (Steubenville, OH: Emmaus Road Publishers, 2021).

(and from) the soul (and the body's being itself is analogous to the soul's possessing existence *per se and* by participation), so too it would seem to follow that the body possesses, as it were, its own distinctive, "bodily" relation to God, which can be distinguished in a certain respect from the soul's immediate relation to God, even though in another respect there is just *one* relation to God of the whole human being.[218] While the implications of this point specifically in relation to the life of the body may seem fairly negligible, at least at first glance,[219] the implications for the political

---

218 We are going beyond Aquinas on this point, but believe we are doing so in fidelity to Thomistic principles. A question has often been raised whether Aquinas does enough justice to the theme of the resurrection of the body (and the role of the body in the beatific vision, which of course would be significantly different if one placed the incarnate Son at the center of that vision).

219 There is no doubt much greater significance than we can explain here, but one can reflect on the place of the body, and matter, in the sacraments, for example, not to mention the theme of the spiritual senses.

order as such stand out fairly sharply, and carry evident importance.

To spell out one of the implications directly here: in communicating God to the city, the Church not only draws the city into the Church's own specific relation to God, the liturgical life of worship with a view to the heavenly kingdom, although it most certainly *does* do that, and this dimension is not a marginal point once we affirm the intrinsic unity between the two orders that we have been elaborating. The Church *also* mediates to the city the city's *own*, *distinctive* relation to God, which is both inseparably related to and yet irreducibly different from the former.[220] In other words, in the light of

220 In this respect, it is interesting to consider the various political theories that arose in the late Middle Ages and early Renaissance, which affirmed the rootedness of political authority in God, but explicitly rejected the Church's mediating role: see Dante's *De Monarchia* or Marilius of Padua's *Defensor Pacis*. The latter text is one of the first truly modern political theories. Our argument is that we must reject the dichotomy: *either* political authority has its roots immediately in God *or* it receives that relation to God

the soul-body analogy, the architectonic status of politics, and the intimate presence of God in *all* human thinking and acting even in its earthly occupations, as we elaborated in chapters one and two, we can say that there is a specifically political role that God plays in the very constitution of the city and its life, which is distinct from (even though at the same time *inseparable* from) the specifically theological/ecclesial role.[221] When

through the Church. Instead, we have to affirm that *both* of these are true (just as the body has its own reality, which in some sense is immediately its own, but at the same time has this reality only by virtue of the soul). This paradoxical affirmation of both at once, incidentally, gives a response to the apparent "tensions" in Aquinas's thought, brought out in the classic discussion of the "two powers": see the classic essay by L. P. Fitzgerald, "St. Thomas Aquinas and the Two Powers," *Angelicum* 56.4 (1979): 515–56.

221 To be very precise: the "natural" and "worldly" presence of Christianity in the city is *also* ecclesial in an analogous sense. In other words, the Church is both an institution that exists in a reciprocal relation to the "world," i.e., the city, in one respect, and is the encompassing *whole* in

hearing of the intersection between religion and politics, we tend, for a variety of reasons, to think first, and perhaps exclusively, of certain moral questions: abortion, issues concerning marriage and family, matters of public decency, and social justice problems. It is of course true that moral questions such as these (if they are indeed ever simply moral questions) are crucial when we speak of God and the city,[222] but if we limit God's significance in the political sphere to such questions, it is arguably one of the clearest signs that we are conceding a

another respect (analogous to the way in which the Church herself is in one respect juxtaposed to Christ as his Spouse and in another respect an extension of Christ as his Body). In the discussion at hand, we are elaborating the first sense, but do not mean to exclude the second.

222 Regarding the relation between morality and God, there persists a debate whether morality is possible without God or not. For a recent expression of this debate (which arguably begins with Plato's *Republic*), see *A Debate on God and Morality*, ed. William Lane Craig, Erik J. Wielenberg, and Adam Lloyd Johnson (New York: Routledge, 2021).

liberal horizon to the political order, which is to say that we are envisioning God and the city as merely extrinsically related, no matter how much *necessity* we wish subsequently to impose on this extrinsic relation. Moral questions, thus conceived, set an external limit to possible human actions— "Thou shalt not" transgress this or that boundary—but they do not need to *inform* human activity positively and from within. A proper interpretation of the religious dimensions of the city recognizes the presence of God, not only outside, but even more profoundly *inside* of human activity, informing it, filling and illuminating its content and inner meaning. If God is the life of the soul, and the soul the life of the body, then God is the life of the life of the body; politically speaking, God is the life of the life of the city. If God is excluded from the political, as the realization of community, the city will be soulless. Or, in fact, because it cannot *help* but have a soul, as a city, it will have something like a functionalized, bureaucratized, immanentized, technologized, mechanized, and so coercively imposed, substitute for a soul. In a word, it will turn diabolical.[223]

To take an example of the positive sense of God as the life of a city: there is nothing more fundamental to a political community than its laws. We tend to think of these as essentially secular in origin, form, and purpose, and as making absolutely no claim regarding the truth of things: they are "merely juridical" rules of play. We might admit, though, that deeper questions come into play if the law concerns explicitly some religious (or moral) matter. But the great legal historian Harold Berman spent a lifetime arguing that law in fact ceases to be law, because it ceases to hold any authority, when it is severed in its exercise, its rituals, its self-understanding and self-presentation, from its original, religious dimension. According to Berman, law, *as* law, by its nature is an expression

223 This is a basic theme of my book *Freedom from Reality: The Diabolical Character of Modern Liberty* (Notre Dame, IN: University of Notre Dame Press, 2017).

willy-nilly of ultimate meaning.[224] It is thus not an accident that, in the ancient Church, the bishop was the judge even in civil matters, and the judgments were pronounced in the basilica, or that, in the Middle Ages, the laws of a city were carved into the walls of its main church.[225] Even law is not a merely juridical matter; laws *as such* are analogously sacred.

To take another example, it was natural for cities to adopt a patron saint, to engage, *as* a city, in the various feasts and fasts, acts of celebration and penance, according to the Church's seasonal, liturgical calendar,[226] to say nothing of the religious meaning of the times that regulated the work of each

---

224 See the important study: Harold Berman, *Law and Revolution: The Formation of the Western Legal Tradition* (Cambridge, Mass.: Harvard University Press, 1983), and *The Interaction of Law and Religion* (Nashville: Abingdon Press, 1974).

225 See *Cities of God*, 120. As Thompson shows, lawyers were in fact sometimes called the priests of the city: 127.

226 See the chapter "The City Worships," in *Cities of God*, 235–71.

day, marked by the church's or monastery's bells.[227] The *festival* lies at the heart of the life of a city. Originally, as Josef Pieper has unforgettably shown, all festivals had a religious dimension, which was often explicit, but nevertheless virtually always present in some respect.[228] But even when the religious dimension is explicit, this does not make the celebration of the festival an ecclesial event in any exclusive way. It is rather a fundamental way of living life in the world; in traditional cultures, all of life *in this world* is organized around such community events. But this means that the enactment of the festivals is the particular responsibility of the *city*, and so of the ruling power. As Christopher Dawson has

---

227 Jacques Le Goff, *Time, Work, and Culture in the Middle Ages* (Chicago: University of Chicago Press, 1982), 48–50; see also the profound reflections on this theme from Gil Bailie in a lecture entitled, "Bells and Whistles: The Technology of Forgetfulness," which can be found online at the Cornerstone Forum.

228 Josef Pieper, *Leisure: The Basis of Culture* (San Francisco: Ignatius Press, 2009), 65–74.

shown, culture is embodied religion[229]; for this to be properly the case, the activities that belong to culture must be recognized as expressing an ultimate meaning, which is to say that their diversity must be made truly alive by being given a soul, or in other words that their diversity must be gathered into a unity, a substantial whole, and this requires the actual representation of the highest human good that constitutes the office of the ruling power.[230] If we tend to think of festivals as a matter of "private" convictions and "private" practices, which constitute civil society *over against* the political order properly speaking, it is because we are unable to think beyond the fragmentation that defines modernity.[231] The very first matter that Plato addresses in his *Laws*, for instance, which is his presentation of codified rule in its ideal form, is how properly to organize a festival,

229 Glenn Olsen elaborates this fundamental idea in "Why We Need Christopher Dawson," *Communio* (Spring 2008): 115–44.

230 On this, see Aquinas, ST 1.103.2ad2.

231 See my essay, "Restoring Faith in Culture," *Communio* (Summer 2021): 223–46.

because he recognized that all of political life turns on this.[232] The festival represents in a paradigmatic way the specifically political face, so to speak, of God, the temporal or secular presence of God in human existence.

Let us in conclusion recall the passage from the *De Regno* with which we began this chapter: the king "is to be in the kingdom what the soul is in the body and what God is in the world." We have been arguing for a genuinely analogical link between these, suggesting that the political authority, on the pattern, so to speak, of the soul's presence to the body, has a privileged role in communicating God's presence to the world. This role is subordinate to the priest's role, and more

---

232 Although the matter of war comes first in the account, Plato (through "the Athenian") points out that war must be conceived as a means to peace, which is the fundamental, and so original, existence of the polis (*Laws* I, 628c-e). He then presents common meals, physical training (games), and drinking parties, as the principal dimension of the formation in the common good that constitutes the life of the city: (*Laws* I, 636a ff.).

broadly, to the Church's role, of course, but to elaborate the relation between these two, we drew on the traditional analogy of the body-soul relation, which Aquinas alludes to elsewhere even if he does not do so directly in this passage of the *De Regno*.[233] To bring this little book to a close, we will reflect on the reason the ruler's presence in the city, after the manner of the soul's presence in the body, is crucial for the analogical role the political order has in "quasi-sacramentally" communicating God's presence in the world. The point, which has a formal and a more concrete and material aspect, can be put simply, but its significance cannot be overstated given our current conceptions. Formally: if there is a genuinely analogical relation among the terms presented, a disorder in one implies a disorder in them all. In this case, governance is present for example only in a mechanical fashion, through elected

233 See Aquinas, *De regno*, I.16 [114-15]. The king is subordinate to the priest, but ought to be interpreted as being charged with making the priest's office effective, so to speak, in the temporal order.

representation calculated more or less quantitatively and through bureaucratic procedures; the city would not be able to be interpreted as a body, but only as a "collocation of atoms." Material elements can *be* a body only by the presence of the soul, which is to say only if there is an actual principle of unity that represents the transcendent good. Charles Péguy once observed that a modern man can become Christian only by first becoming pagan, because there has to be a soul there to convert, and modern man has no soul.[234] A similar thing can be said about a city, which can be Christian only if it in truth has a soul. In a liberal democracy, God could not communicate his presence by analogy to the soul, because there would be no intrinsically unified body to in-form in such a way. But it is not only the God-world relation that is mediated by the king-kingdom relation; the body-soul relation in the individual man also, perhaps less obviously but no less profoundly, depends on this. A distorted sense

234 Charles Péguy, "Clio I," in *Temporal and Eternal* (Indianapolis: Liberty Press, 2001), 161.

of political order will affect even one's own sense of one's reality. We cannot explore the matter here, but it bears remarking that, for example, the very thinkers who reconceived political order fundamentally in non-traditional forms, and who conceived God principally as *force*, either inside of or outside the political order as such—Hobbes and Locke—were also champions of a mechanistic science, specifically in relation to the human body.

With this observation we are already entering into the concrete formulation of the point: as we have seen, the ruling power *cannot but* represent, and be responsible for, "the highest good to the highest degree." It is not possible for God to enter into the world, and certainly not into human existence, without some relation to "the highest good to the highest degree" that belongs in a constitutive way to the *res publica*. Instead, God can enter only in some respect *as* the highest good in the highest degree, which means he appears, so to speak, as *revealing* the essence of that highest good, as interpreting it, as summing up in himself its essential content. Moreover, this perfection includes communicating his goodness to others, and in a special way to the ruling power, who communicates it effectively to the people.[235] But if it is the office of the ruling power to *represent* that good, and so to communicate the presence of God, it follows that he will inevitably, and perhaps in spite of all intentions, determine in an official, and so *real*, manner the way God appears in human existence, setting in some sense the horizon for the way God is able to be received specifically by "the people," and for that reason by the individuals who are members of the community.[236]

---

235 See Aquinas ST 1.103.6.

236 In this respect, Heidegger is not wrong to say that we cannot properly relate to God without in some sense first evoking a sense of the holy, which requires us to understand being aright: see "Letter on Humanism," 242. This point can be extended to include the necessity of a political order properly set on what is good. But Jean-Luc Marion is also correct to criticize Heidegger on this point (see "The Crossing of Being," in *God Without Being: Hors-Texte* [Chicago: Chicago University Press, 1991], 53-107) for allowing philosophy to set the "conditions of the possi-

It may help illustrate the point if we consider an obvious objection. One might point to the fact that people have experiences of God, sometimes trivial or sentimental, but other times profound and radically life-altering, which have *nothing* to do with politics or the community, and certainly not with whomever happens to be the ruling power: one often has such experiences walking in nature, precisely *outside* the city walls, or in a church, or perhaps in the privacy of one's home, in a dream, through a chance encounter, and so forth. These are evidently

bility" of God's appearance to man in a one-sidedly *a priori* way. Nevertheless, Marion is wrong to posit relation to God therefore simply outside of, or prior to, man's relation to being, just as it would be wrong to make the relation to God, which transcends the political sphere, something that occurs prior to or outside of the political sphere. Relation to God is always mediated by metaphysics and politics, even if that mediation is a paradoxical one that gives priority to relation to God. On all of this, see Ferdinand Ulrich, *Homo Abyssus* and "Politische Macht," as well as my *Politics of the Real* and *Catholicity of Reason.*

non-political experiences. In fact, it would be quite difficult to conceive of any well-known conversion experience happening specifically *in* and *as a result of* the "public square." Is this not a decisive refutation of the claim that has just been made about the role of the ruling power in the reality of God? The answer is *no*; it only seems so because the examples are considered in abstraction. The point of the claim is that a community is a reality, and as such has an order, which is realized in and through the governing principle or ruling power; this community, the city, establishes the basic horizon of human existence, the life of man as a rational, and therefore political, animal. If this is a liberal horizon, which is to say if the horizon is essentially circumscribed by the assumption that politics is a purely secular order, which at its best (from a religious perspective) clears space for the faith life of individuals, and to a certain limited extent, institutions, conceived as functions of private conviction, then insofar as one has relationships with reality or any other human being, which is to say insofar as one is actually human, that experience of God will be allotted a particular *place* in one's life, the boundaries of which are set by the liberal political institution. The God one has encountered in the woods, then, has to stay in the woods. And, indeed, in a liberal horizon, as *opposed to* a pre-modern political horizon, which is founded on human *nature*, and so which has a constitutive relation to the natural, the woods themselves, so to speak, cannot have an essential bearing on the life in common, on the city. It may be true that, in the secret depths of one's heart, one has experienced this God as life-giving, as the key to human happiness, as the ultimate savior of the world, as the supreme truth and authority over all things—but in a liberal order one can actually believe all of this only as long as one recognizes and respects the fact that others do not experience God in this way, and so the official acknowledgment of the truth of God cannot be an essential part of the political order in which the liberal man lives. God can be "true for me," but not true with respect to history, to the actual created order of nature, and to the natural order of politics, the economy, and social life that constitutes the *reality* and the *identity* of the city. No matter how sublime and awesome this God is, he is impotent in relation to the ruling power, who has neutralized God's possible claim to truth precisely by confessing in a systematic way his incompetence, as a statesman, in religious matters.[237] Here we see quite clearly how the ruling power willy-nilly mediates the presence of God in human existence.

But we can approach this same point more positively. It is the nature of authority to be *generative* of what is other than the original source, as the very word implies: "auctoritas" comes from "auctor," author, and even more fundamentally from "augere," to augment or make grow. All authority comes from God, says St. Paul. We might add that this "coming from" is itself an expression, a fruit, of authority. The authority of the Father most perfectly implies the authority of the Son; the authority of the Son, the authority

237 See my chapter, "The Merely Political Common Good: On the Totalitarianism of Incompetence," *Politics of the Real*, 69–105.

of his body, the extension of the incarnation in space and time which is the Church; the authority of the Church implies the political authority, which implies the distinct and irreducible authority in every particular sphere of human existence. This self-diffusing analogy of authority does not compromise the supreme authority of God, in the sense that "sharing" authority would mean a diminution of the source. Instead, it is the amplification of the source, through the different orders of being. Authority, in this sense, is a life-line, a communication of being.[238] If the ruling power does indeed enact the role of "standing for" the highest good in the highest degree, he gives rise to a city that is fully alive, and fully human. The order generated by authority is not a dead order, which gives signs of life only by provoking the micro and macro acts of rebellion of otherwise detached and private units. In *symbolically* giving life, the ruling power is everywhere, as Aquinas says, throughout the

238 See my essay, "Sources of Authority," *New Polity* (Spring 2022): 17-23.

city, even where physically absent. Our suggestion is that, in being present himself thus, the ruler makes the Church present, the Church makes Christ present, and Christ reveals the Father. The glory of God is the city fully alive.

If, by contrast, we insist that the ruling power does *not* have this role; that he is only a single citizen like the others in a modern democracy, and so he rules not according to the organic analogy of the soul in the body, but according to the mechanical model of the bureaucratic statesman, it means there is no political authority properly speaking, however forceful the power may remain.[239] But if there is no genuine political authority, it means the ruler does not communicate the

239 Here we see the gross failure of the contemporary versions of "integralism" that think it is possible to restore order simply by subordinating the state, in its modern form, to the "authority" of the Church: see, for example, the essay by one of the editors of the integralist website, *The Josias*, Jonathan Culbreath, "The Modern State Is a Good—May It Be Christian," *New Polity* (February 2021): 44–53.

life that he receives, so to speak, from above. But this means there is no Church authority properly speaking, and this is a denial, an enacted rejection, of the authority of God in Jesus Christ. A modern liberal democratic political order is incompatible in principle with life in the Church, which becomes especially clear once we recognize that Christian life is meant to embrace the whole of human existence, and not only in its eschatological aspiration, but in its full temporal unfolding.[240]

240 Note that there can be an interpretation of democracy *distinct from* the soulless modern version: for example, in the work of G. K. Chesterton, who loved democracy because he loved Christ and the Church.

Conclusion

In chapter one, we argued that God enters inevitably, if not directly, into every political order, since politics, as the architectonic practical science, is essentially concerned with the highest good to the highest degree.

In chapter two, we argued that God enters politics in and through man, who is constitutively related to God in the order both of essence and of operation, and who possesses his nature always *politically*, that is, as shared in actual community.

In chapter three, we characterized the form of God's presence to the city as analogous to the soul's relation to the body, and suggested that this analogy is mediated specifically in and through the ruling power. Through authority, ontologically conceived, God gives life to the city.

The political nihilism that dominates the contemporary horizon has provoked in some circles anxious calls for a return to religion, and for a revival of "integralism," at least as a thought experiment. But it is not enough to juxtapose political theology, on the one hand, to an empty political science, on the other. What we need is a genuinely philosophical mediation, which is what we are proposing here as a political metaphysics. In other words, we need to recall a much more robustly human sense of politics, a recognition that the political order represents the highest mode of being in its created reality in the cosmos. It has been traditionally recognized that (Greek) metaphysics concerns, not just a part, but the *whole* of reality, without exception[241]; it has also been recognized that the (Jewish) relation to God concerns the whole of existence, and not just the explicit practices of worship.[242] But we arguably have yet to appreciate adequately the way the *polis*,

---

241 See, for example, Josef Pieper, "The Philosophical Act," in *Leisure: The Basis of Culture.*
242 For an interesting reflection on this from a philosophical perspective, see Sanford L. Drob, "Judaism as a Form of Life," in *Tradition: A Journal of Orthodox Jewish Thought*, 23.4 (Summer 1988): 78–89.

the (Roman) political dimension of human existence, also concerns the whole of reality, and not just coercive power and the legal regulation of public behavior. We have not yet sufficiently recognized that Christianity is a "whole of wholes," gathering up these three dimensions—the Greek, the Jewish, and the Roman—without compromising any one of these in its proper order, and thus giving glory to God, who, in Christ, has become "all in all [τὰ πάντα ἐν πᾶσιν]" (Col 3:11).[243]

The need for a "politics of the real" is especially evident when the bracketing of faith claims in the public square, which has justified itself as a prudential remedy for violence, has turned into a systematic rejection of any official acknowledgment of the truth and destiny of the human person simply. The

---

243 The context of this phrase is significant: "In Christ there is no Greek and Jew, circumcised and uncircumcised, barbarian, Scythian, slave and free; but Christ is all and in all." Paul also explains that Christ "is before all things and in him all things hold together": Col 1:17. All things have their integrity in community, in Christ.

absence of truth as the foundation of politics has generated a much more pervasive violence, which has entered even into our own self-conception, dividing person from nature, the soul from the body, unto the marrow of our bones. The point of a "political metaphysics" is to recall that politics is *always* and *inevitably* at its core an establishing in reality of claims about ultimate meaning, claims about truth, goodness, and beauty. If the Church is to communicate God's presence in the world, it is not only to save man's soul, but also his body. Understood as a body-soul unity, man is essentially connected to this world, and to others in this world, so that we may say that the Church exists, in part, so that the city might have life, and have it in abundance.